Iceland Pictorial

Iceland Pictorial

Rob Benton

Esotericom®

All photographs by Rob Benton

ISBN 978-0-9710702-8-8

And God walked, and where He trod
His footsteps hollowed the valleys out
And bulged the mountains up.
....
The lakes cuddled down in the hollows of the ground,
And the rivers ran down to the sea;
And God smiled again,
And the rainbow appeared,
And curled itself around His shoulder.
....
And God said, "That's good!"

--from The Creation, by James Weldon Johnson

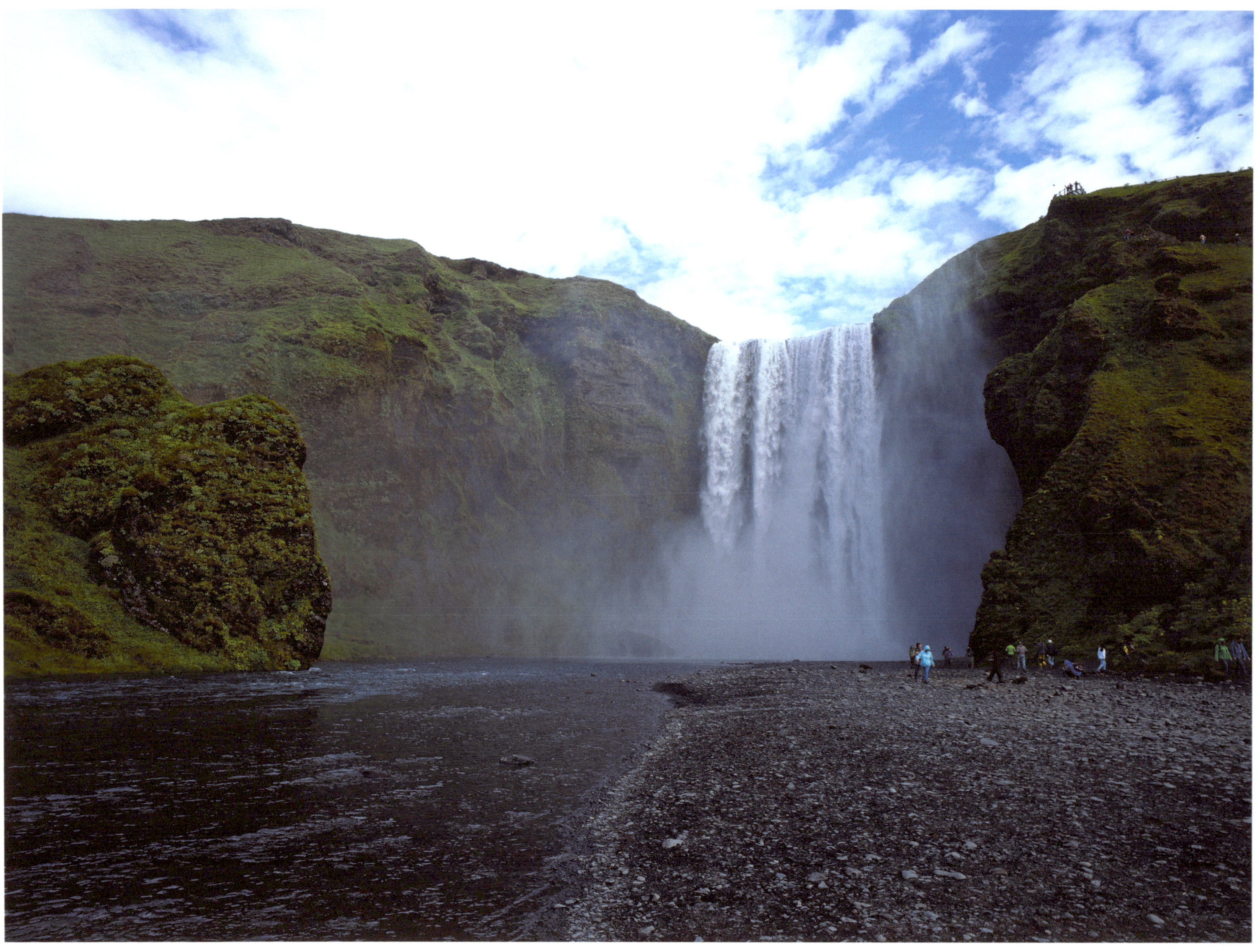

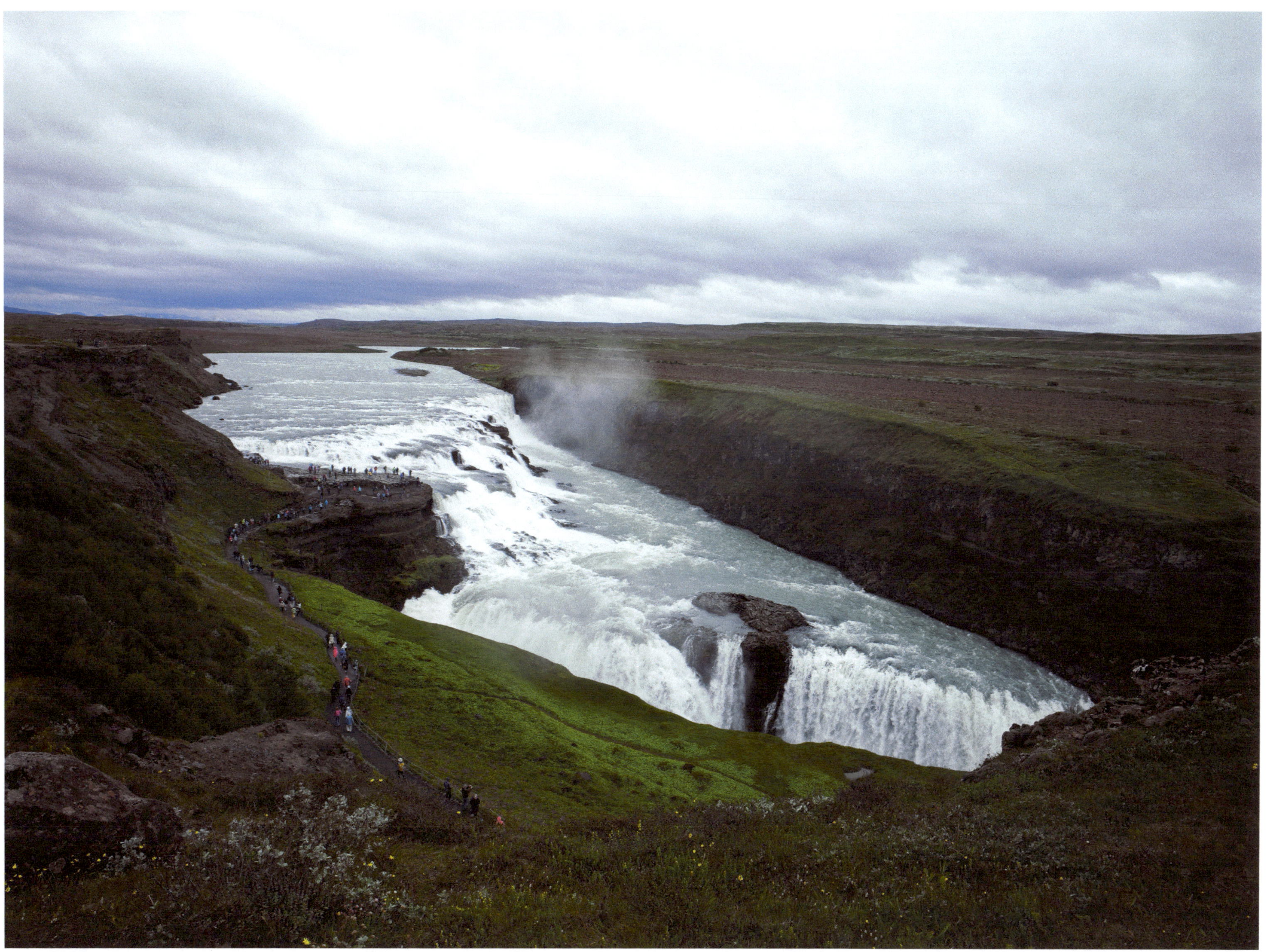

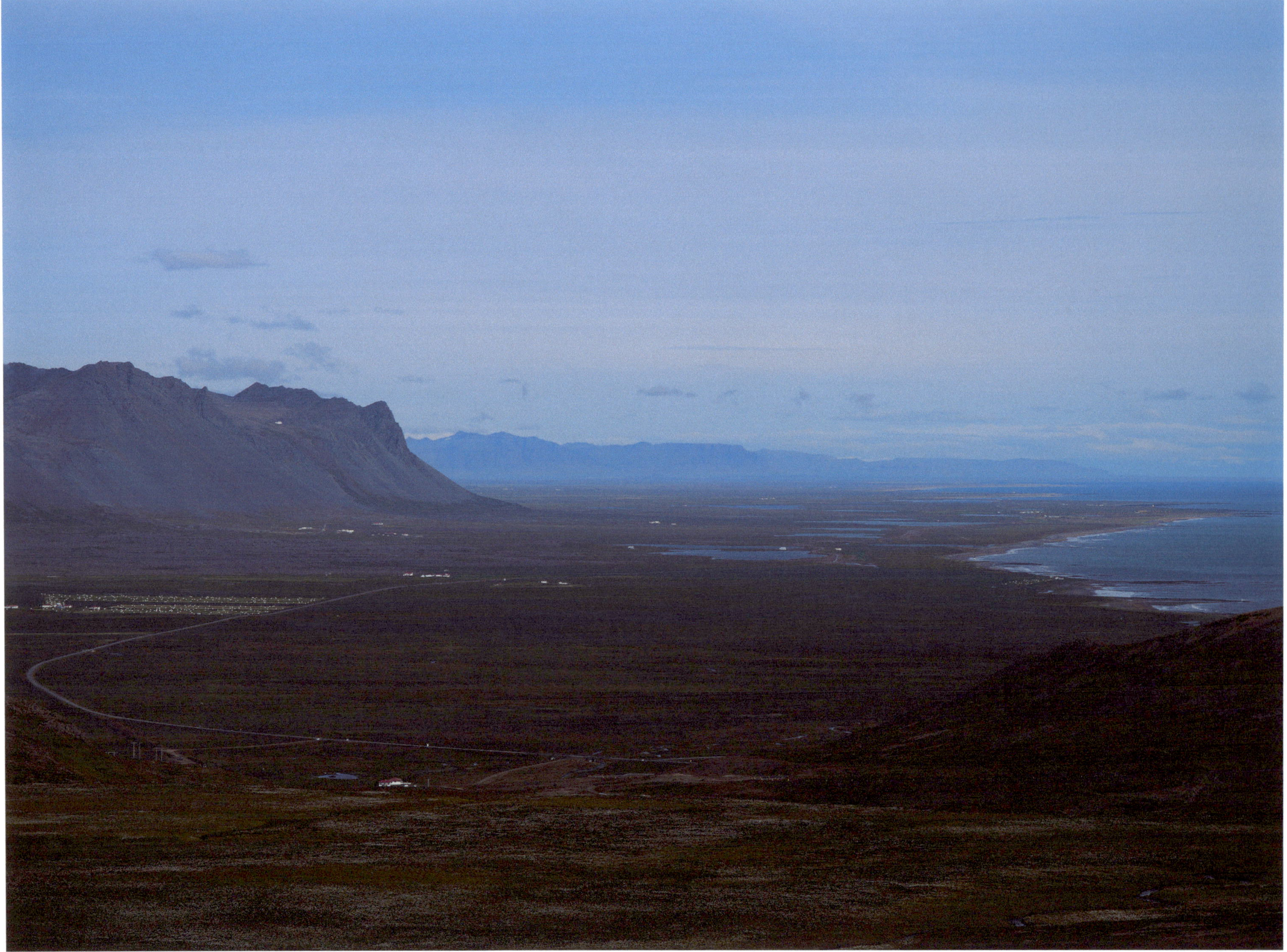

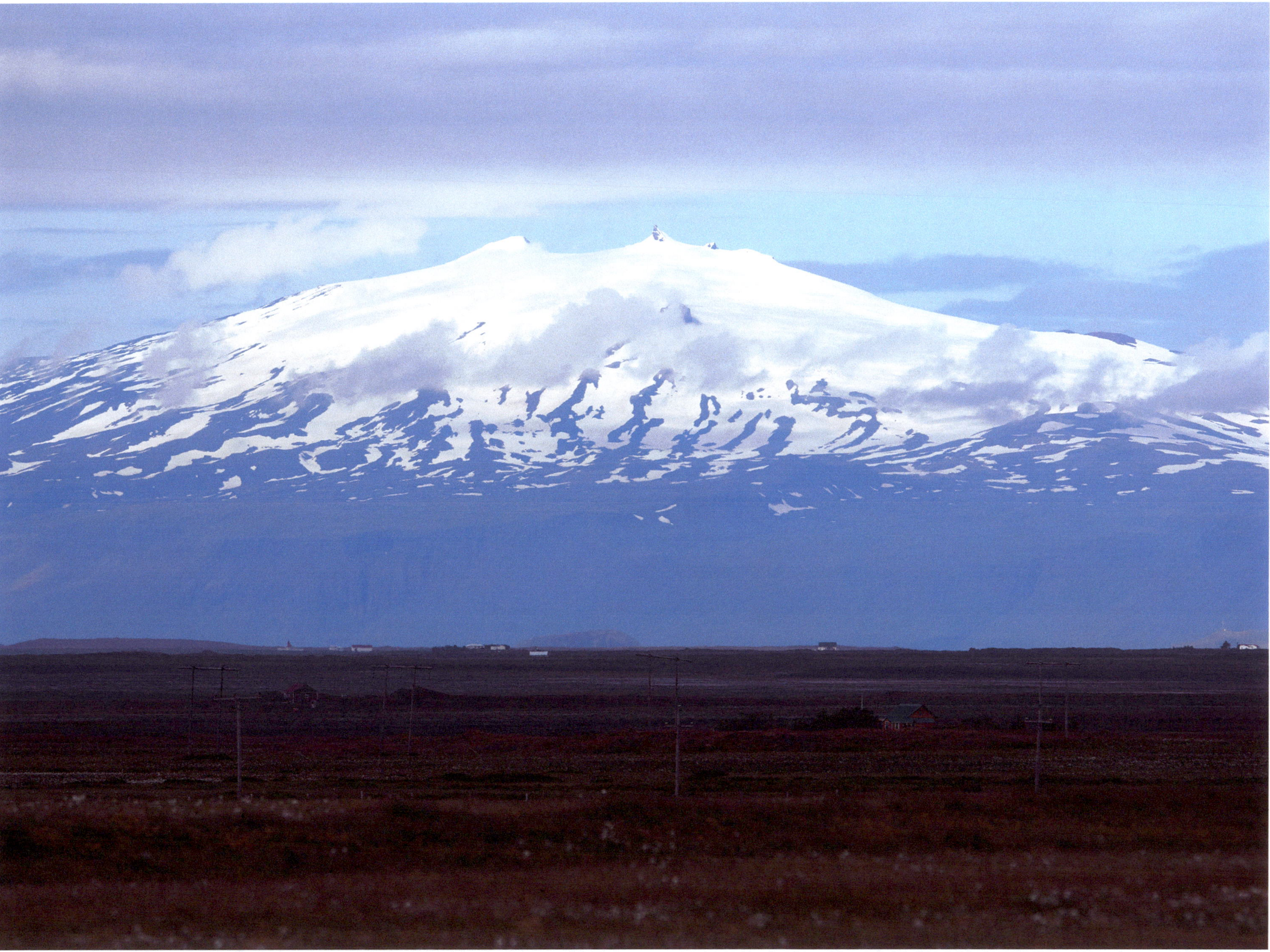

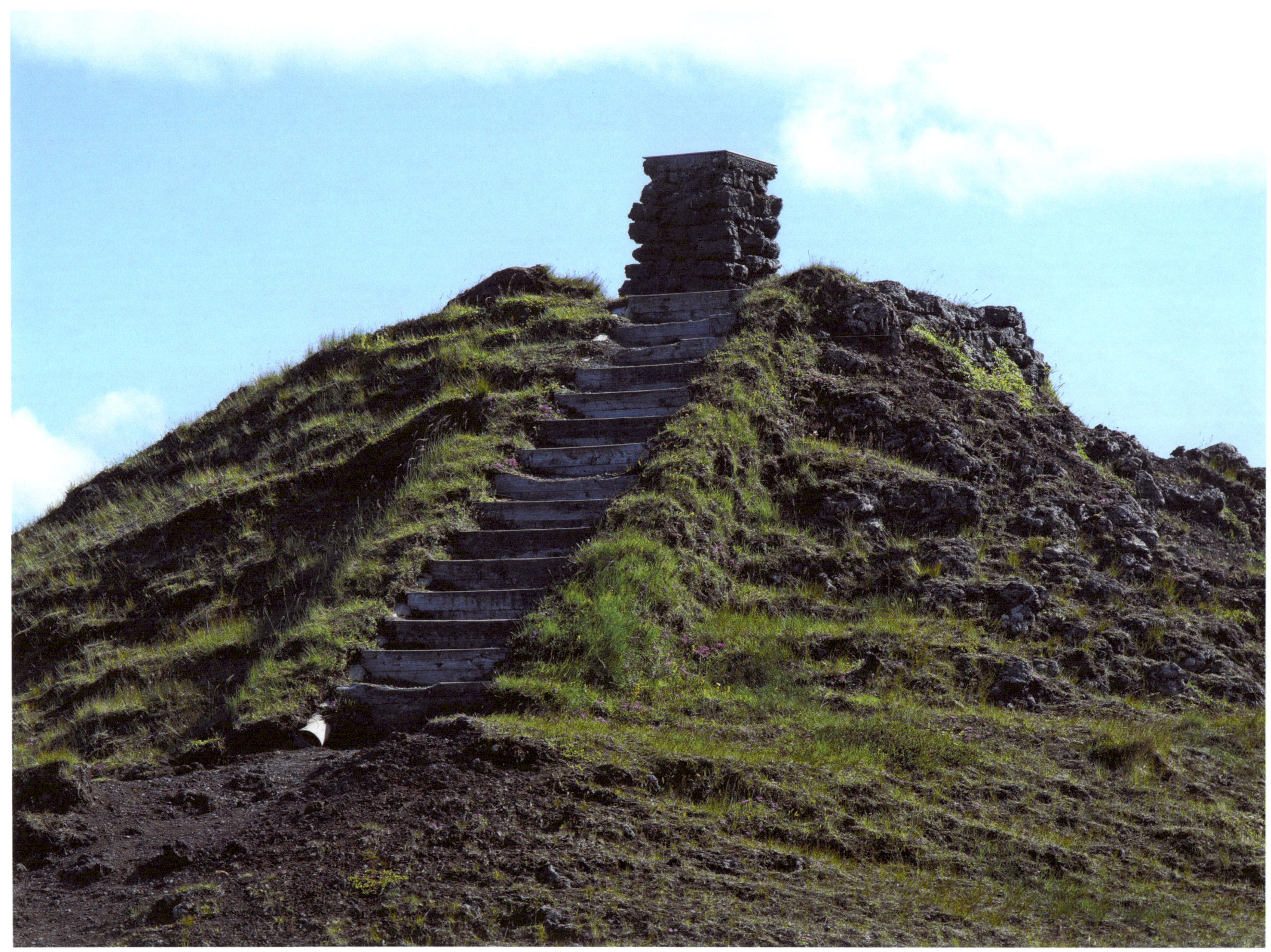

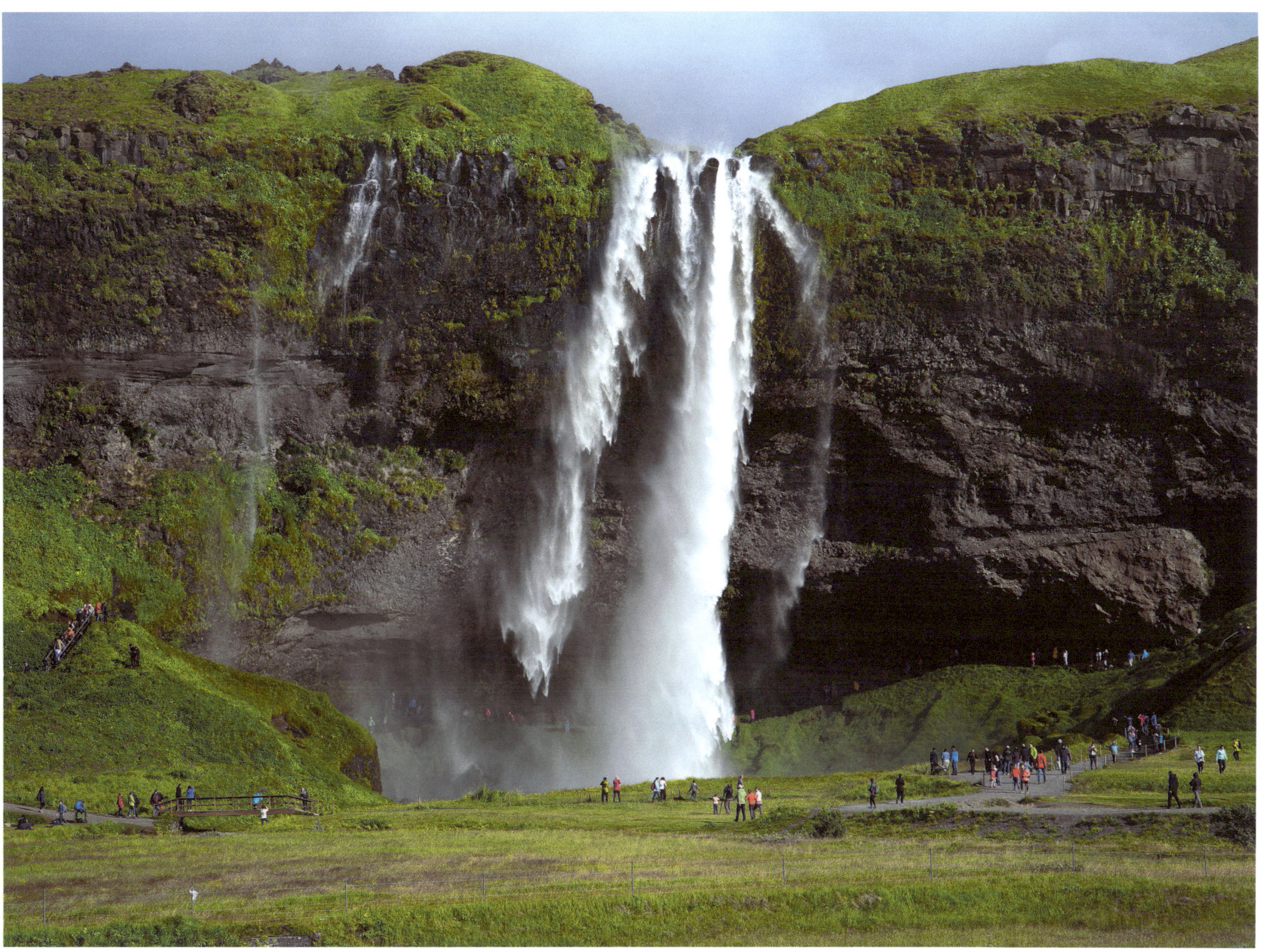

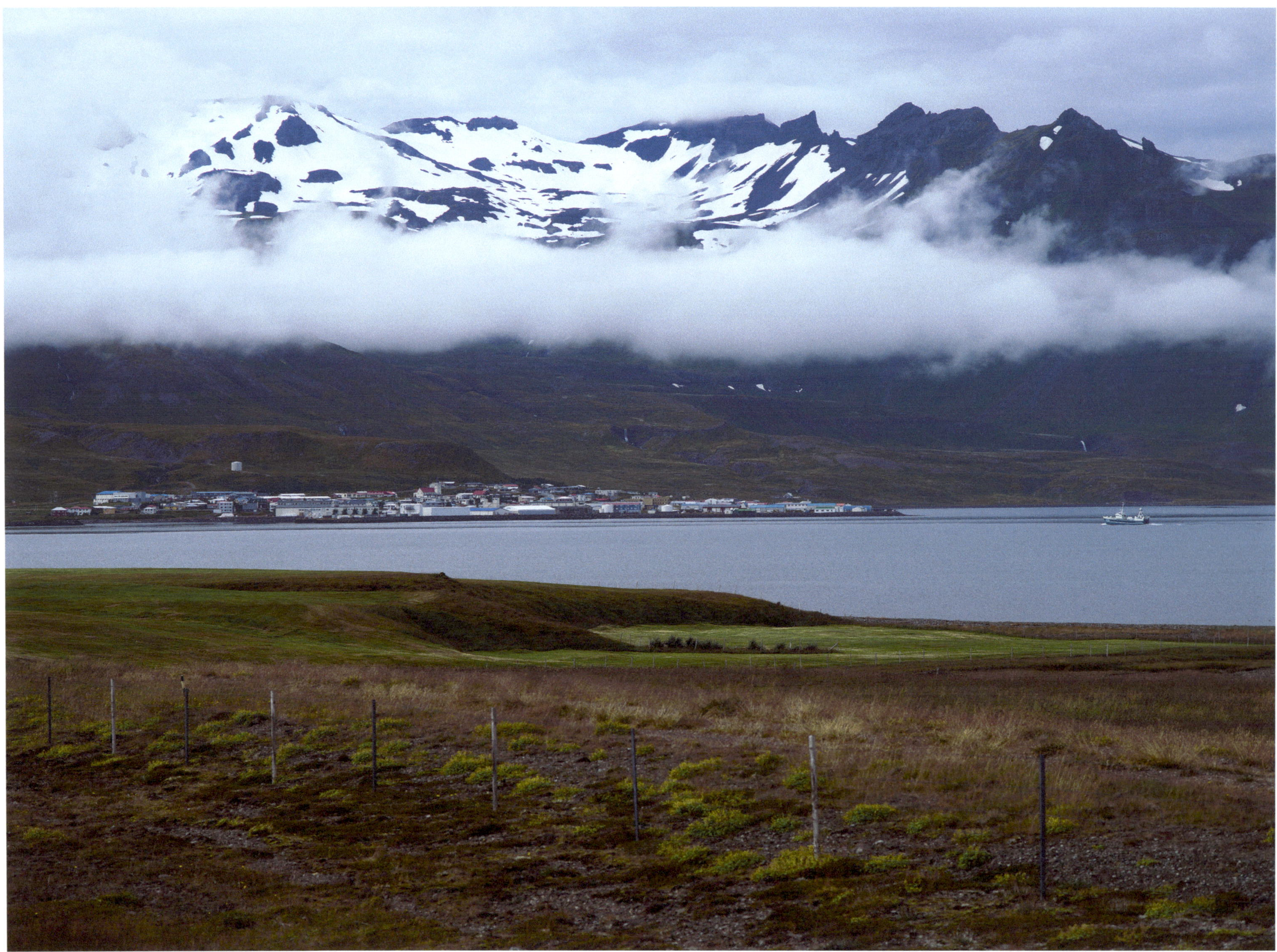

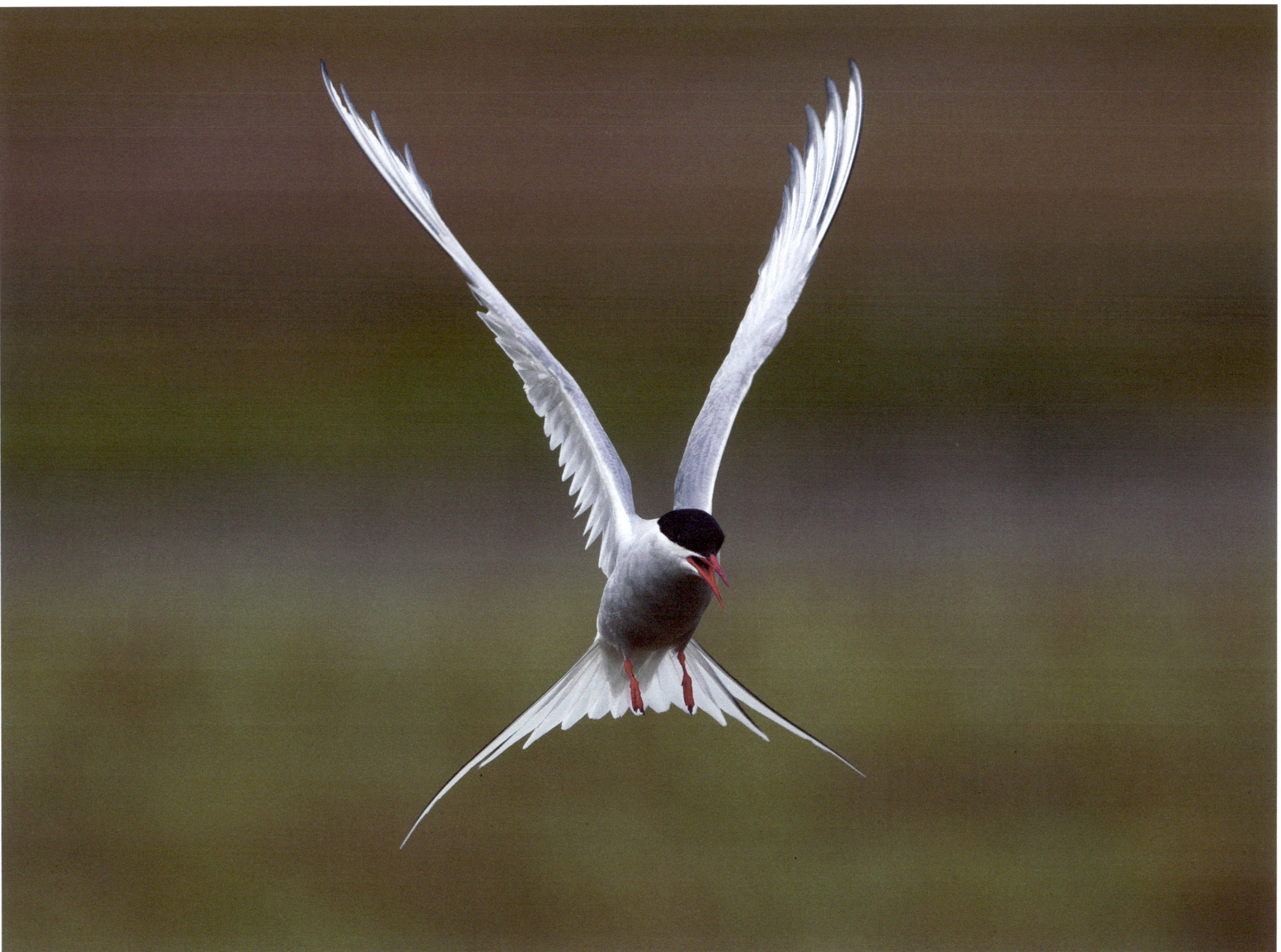

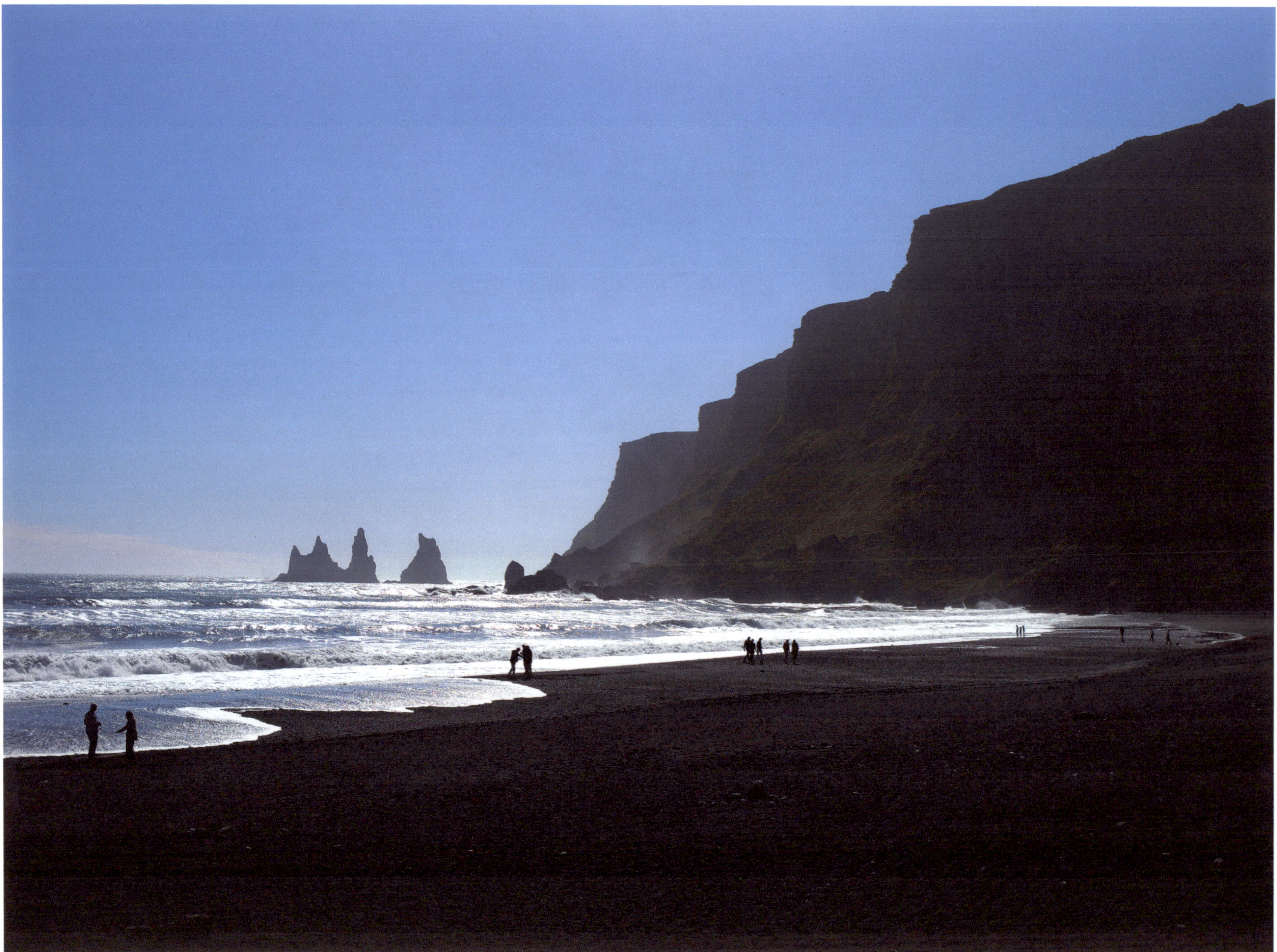

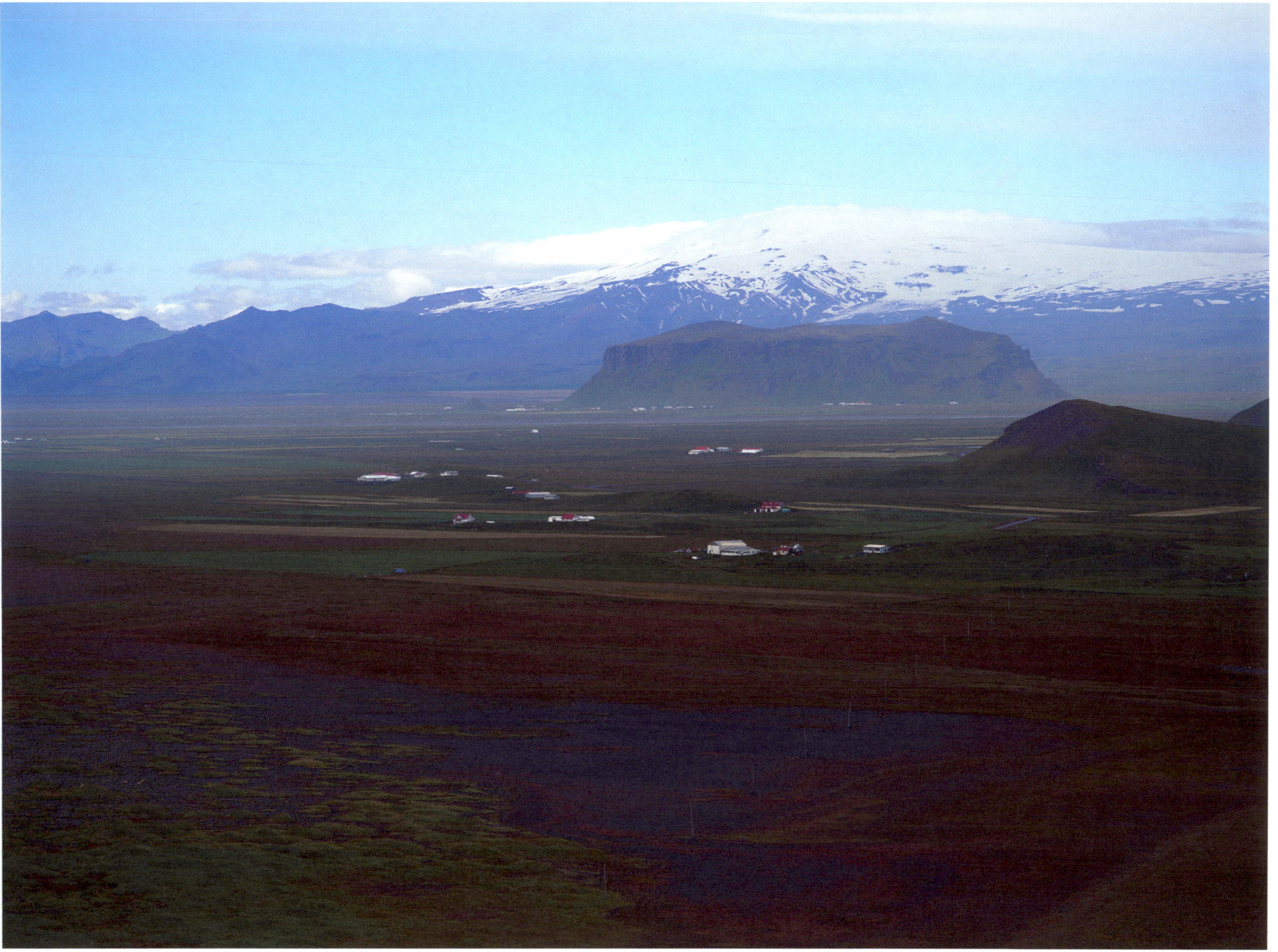

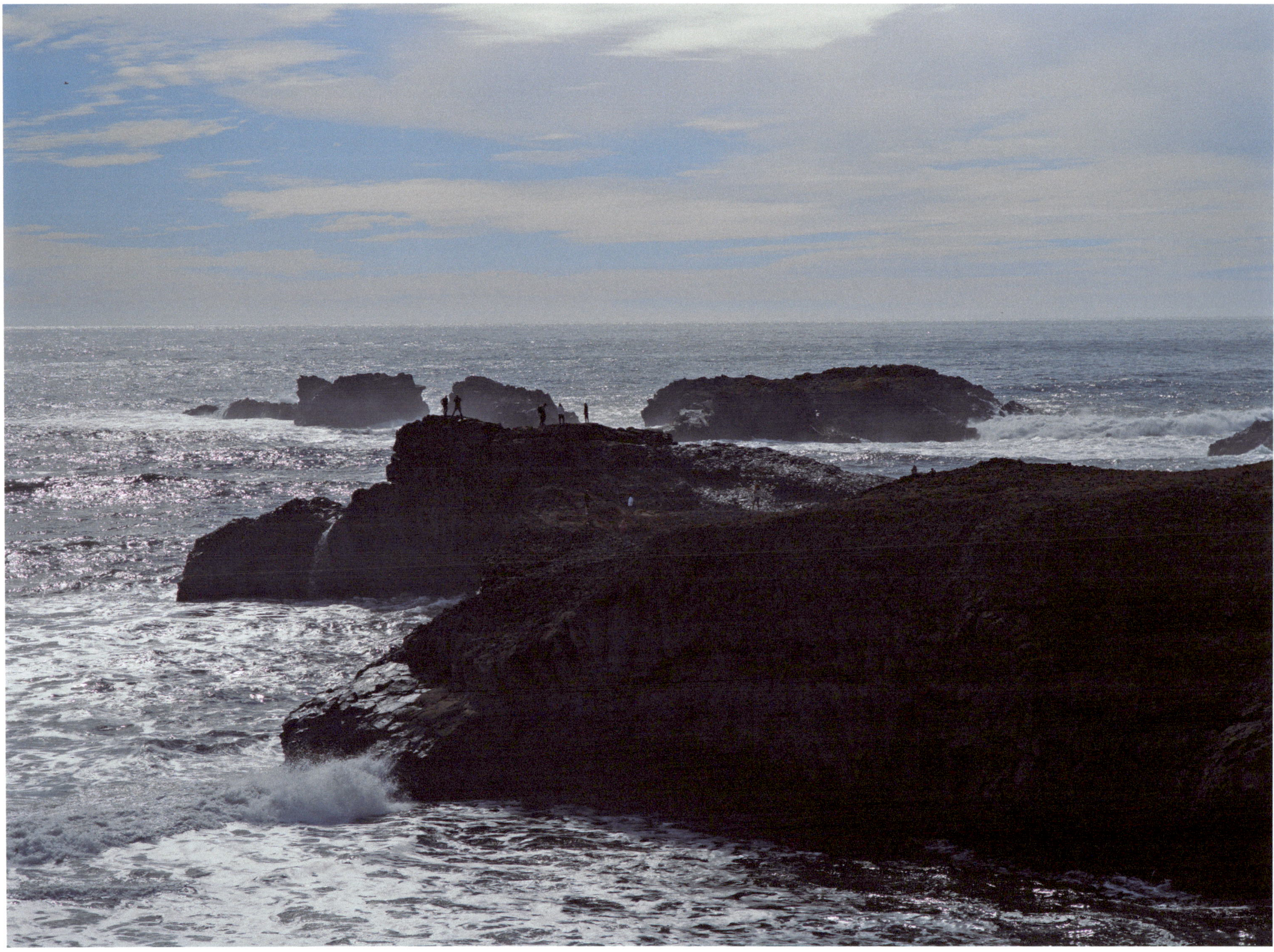

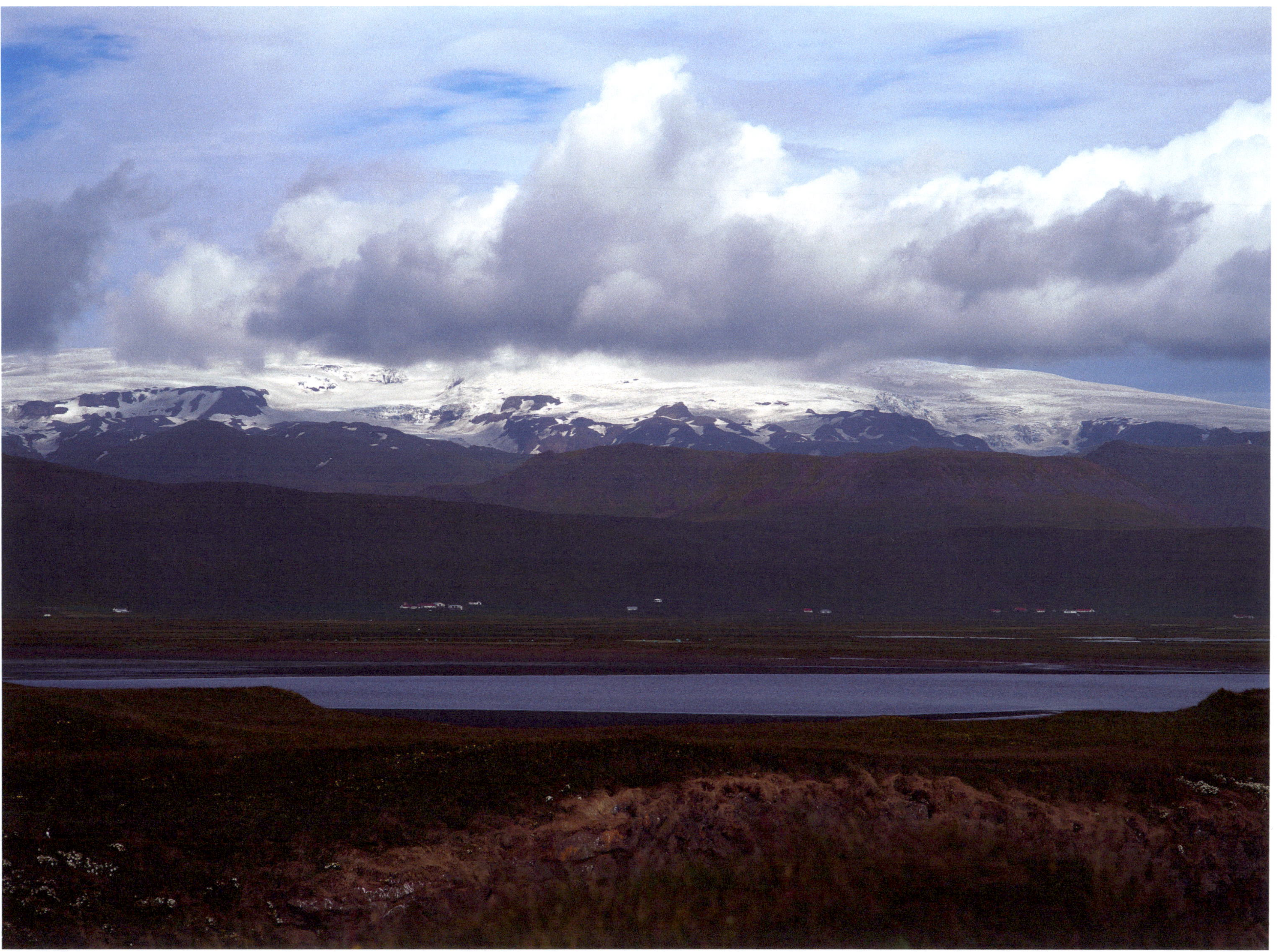

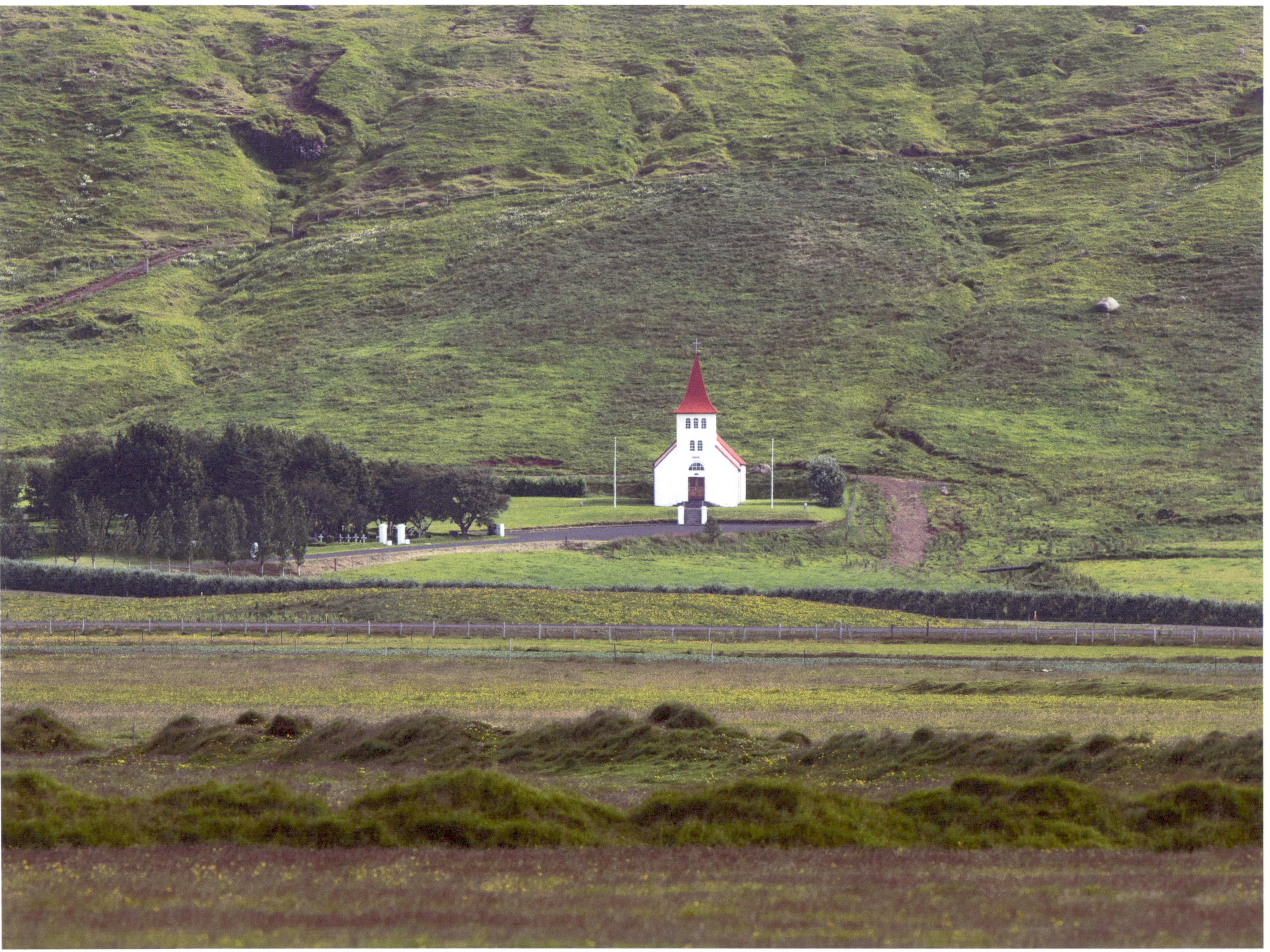

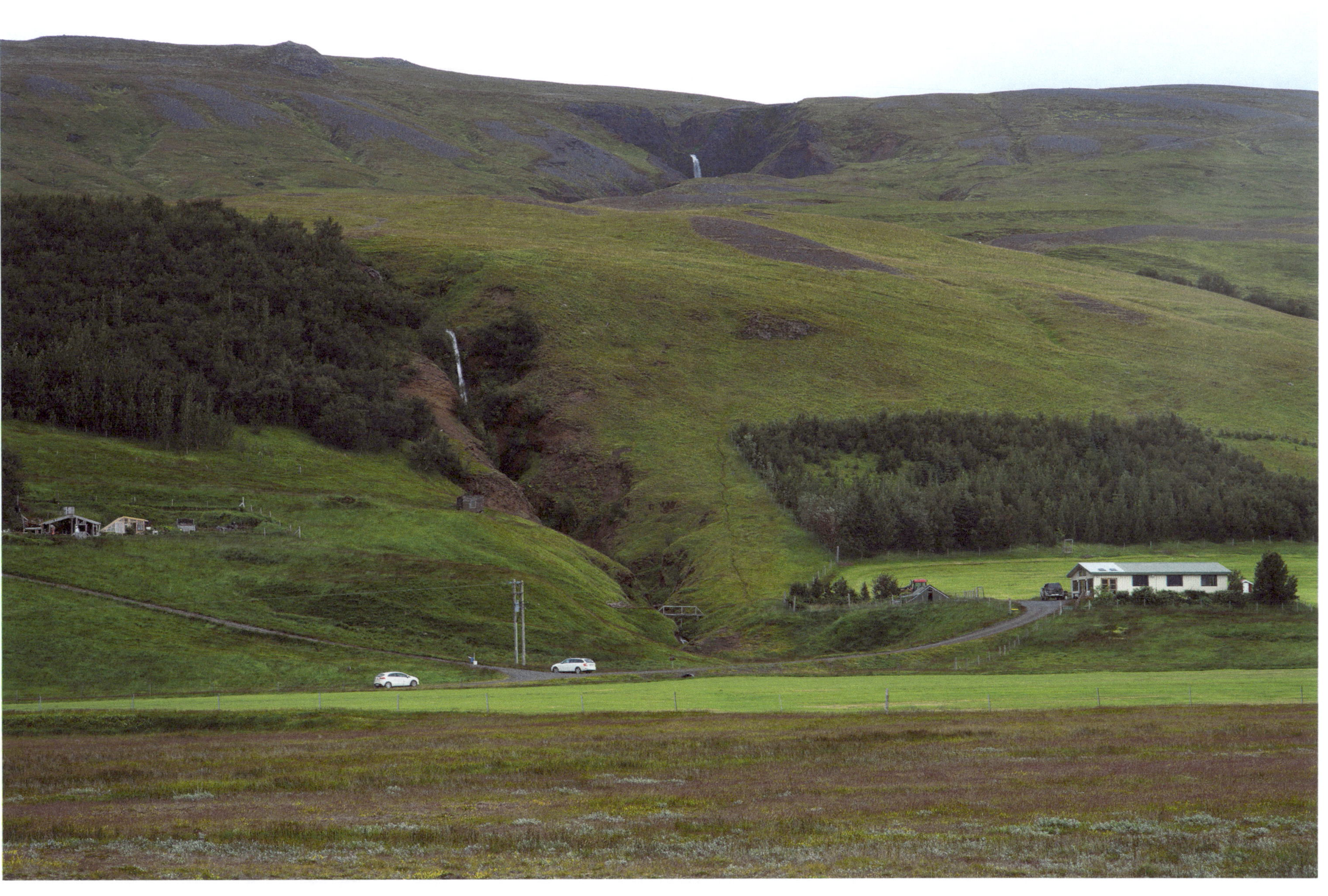

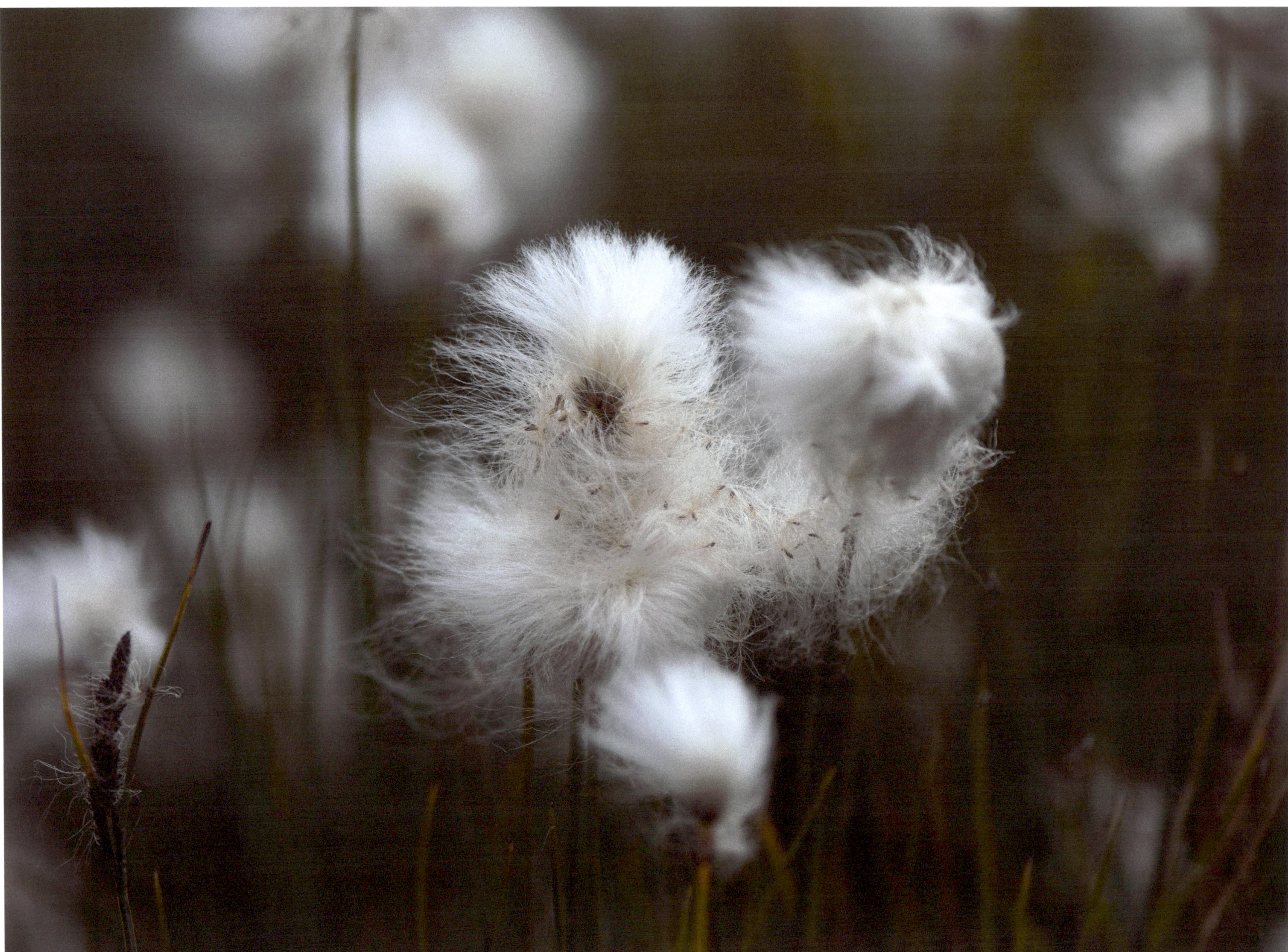

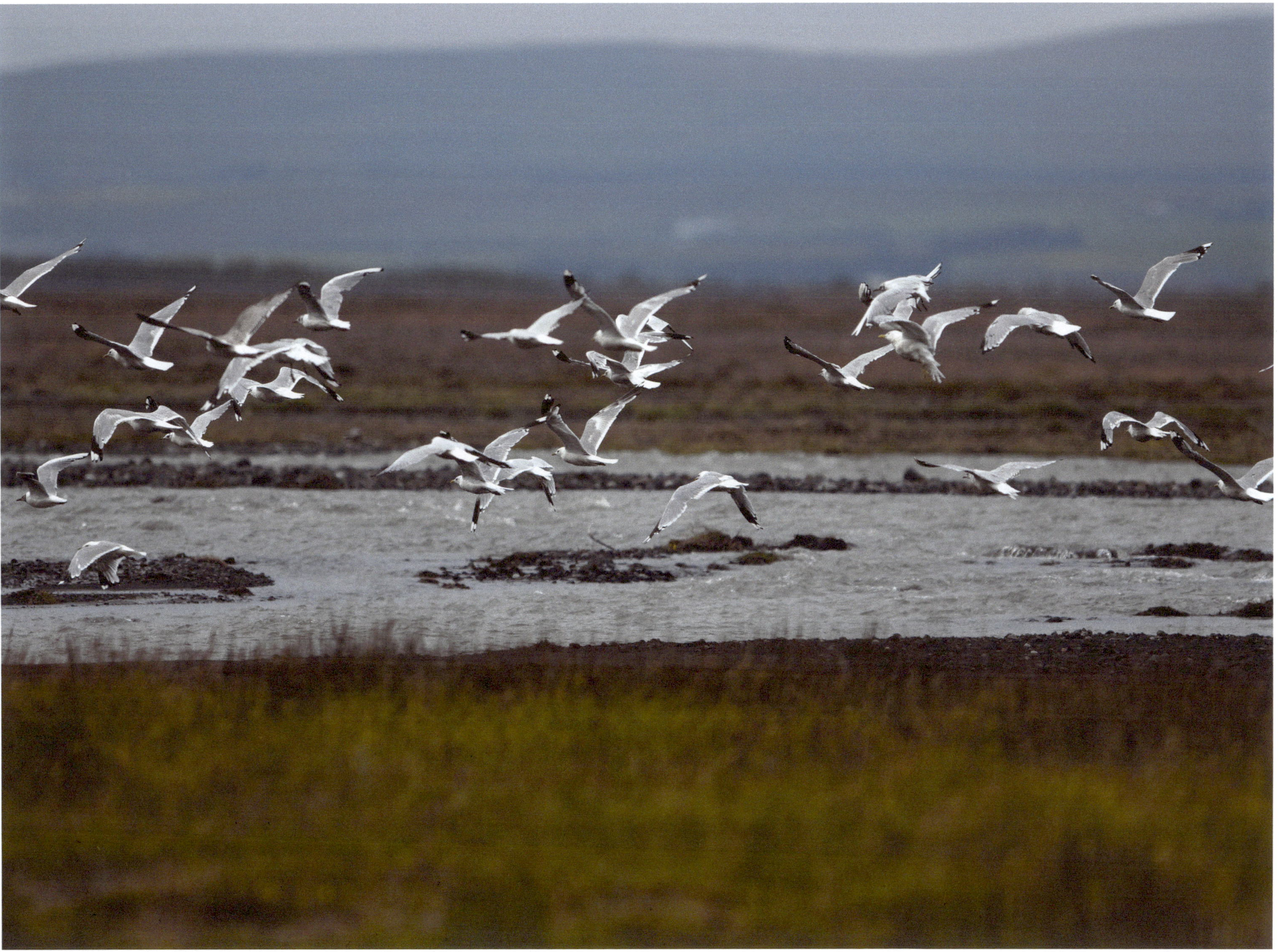

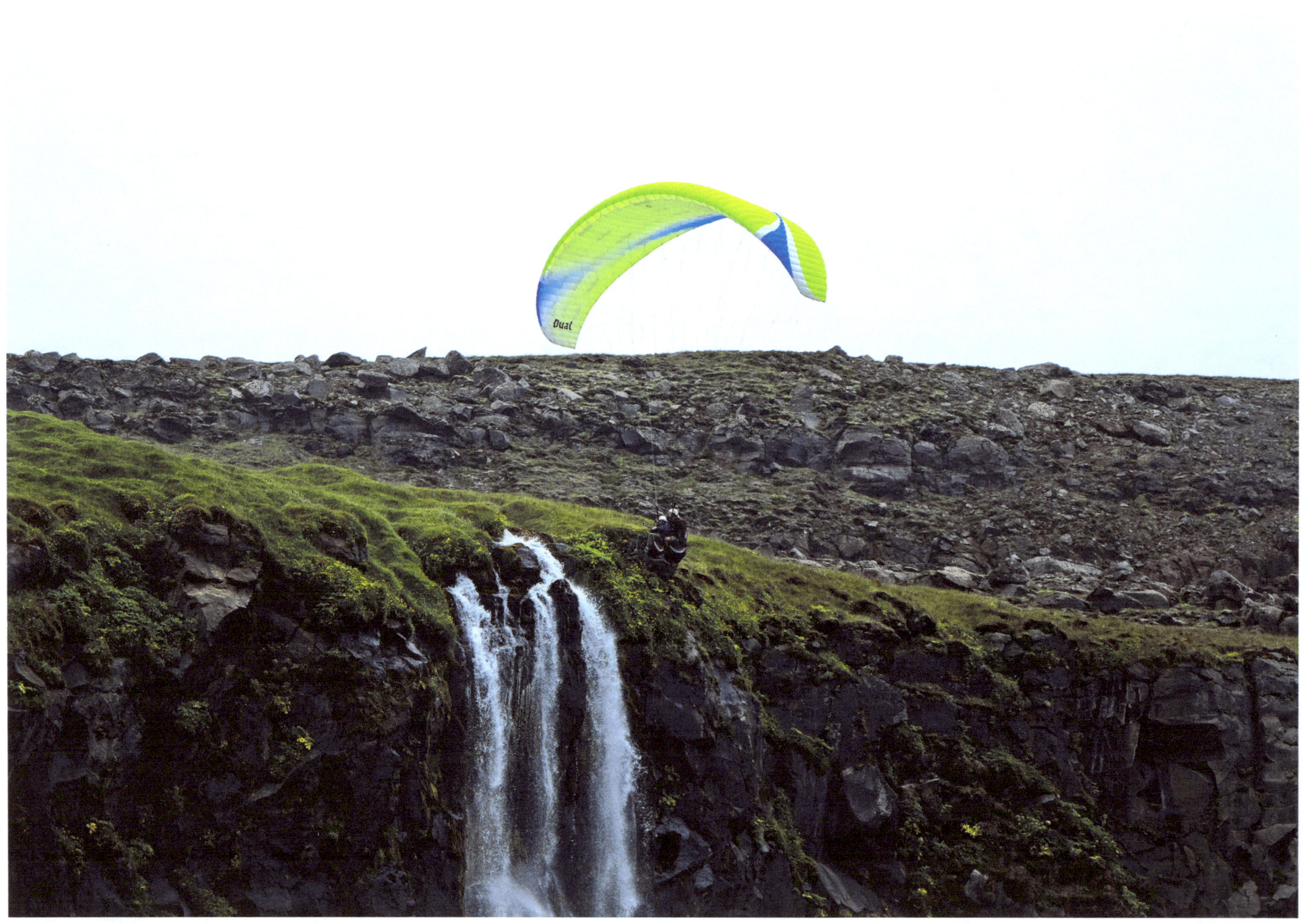
Dual

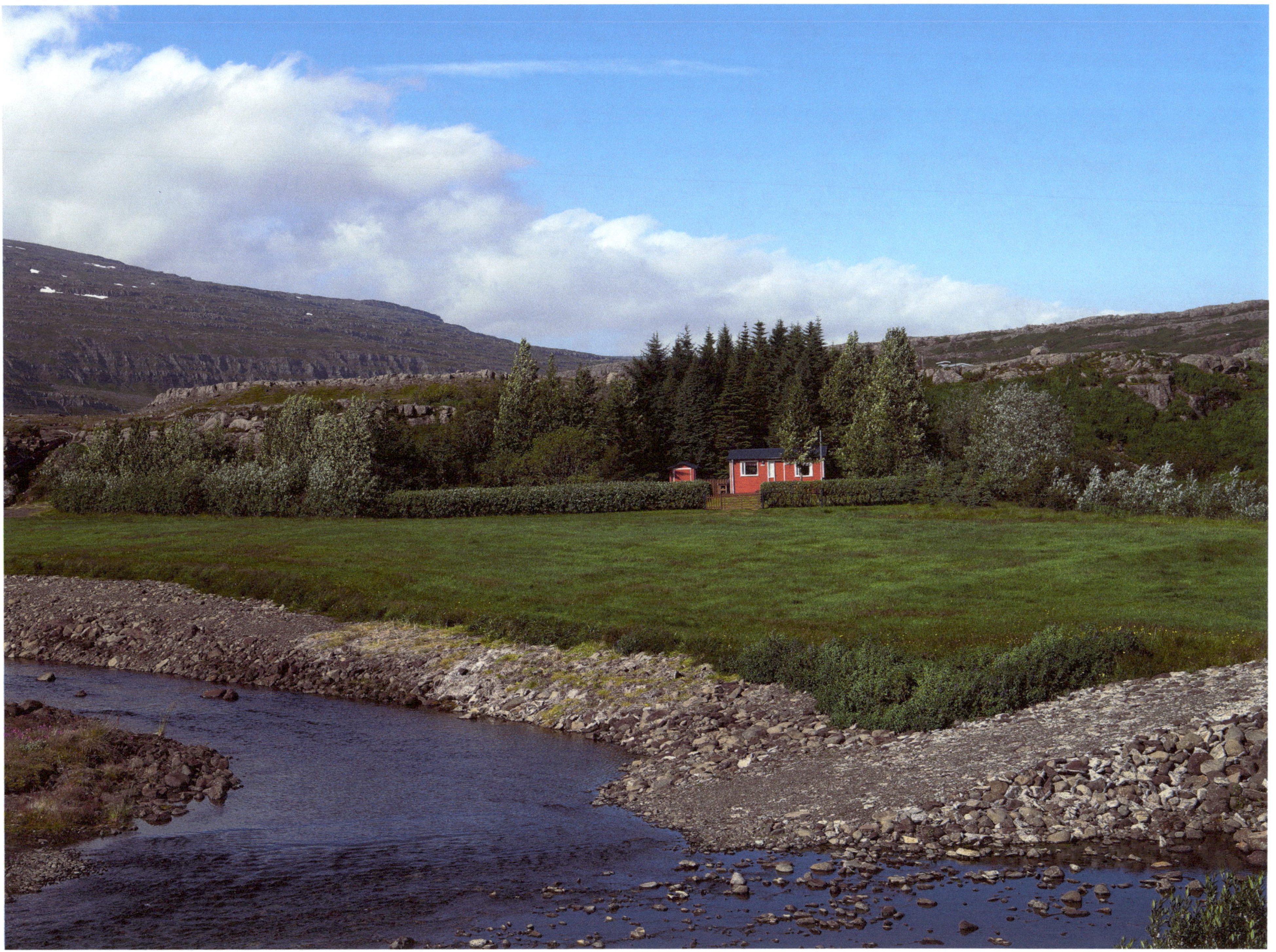

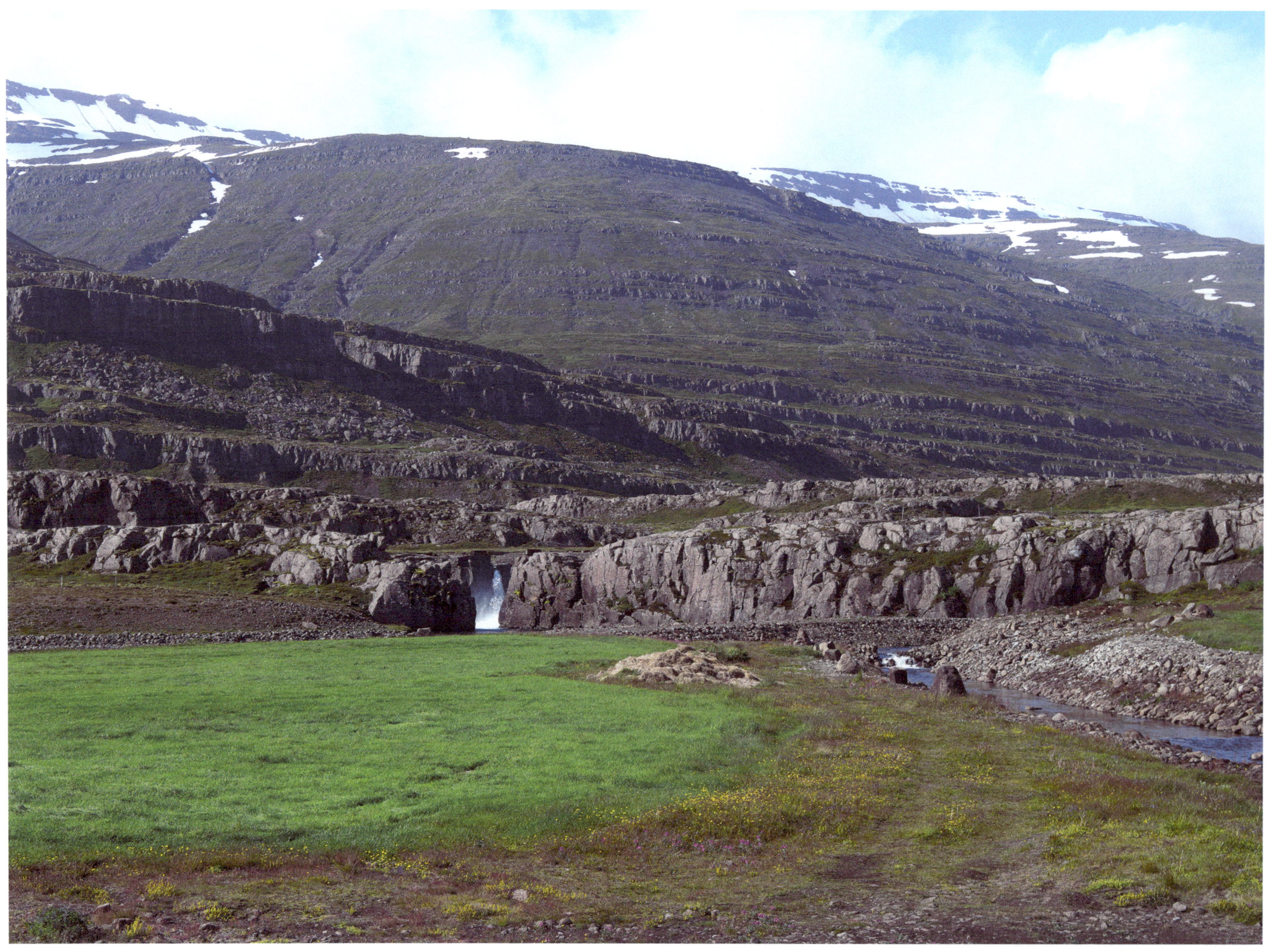

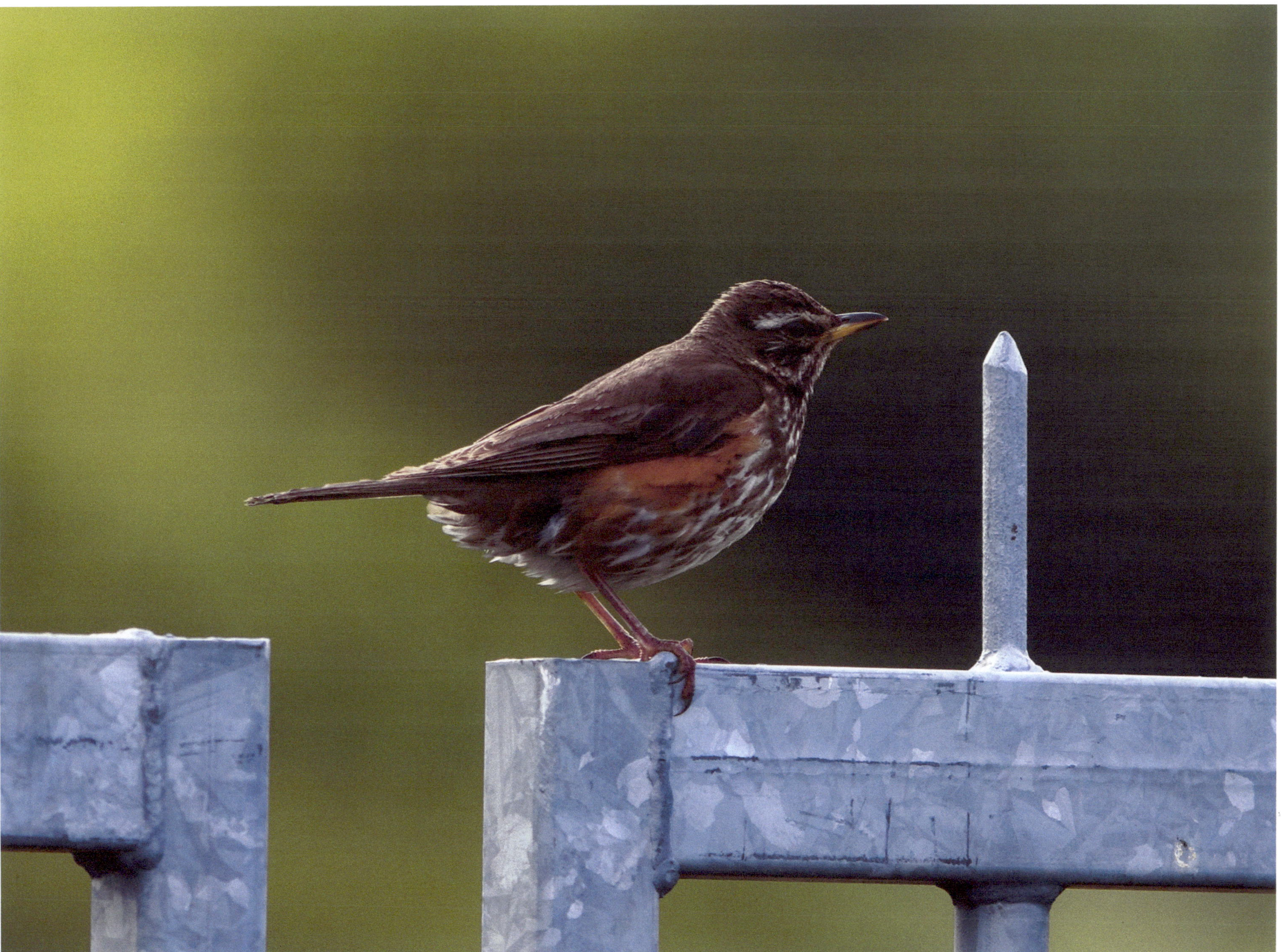

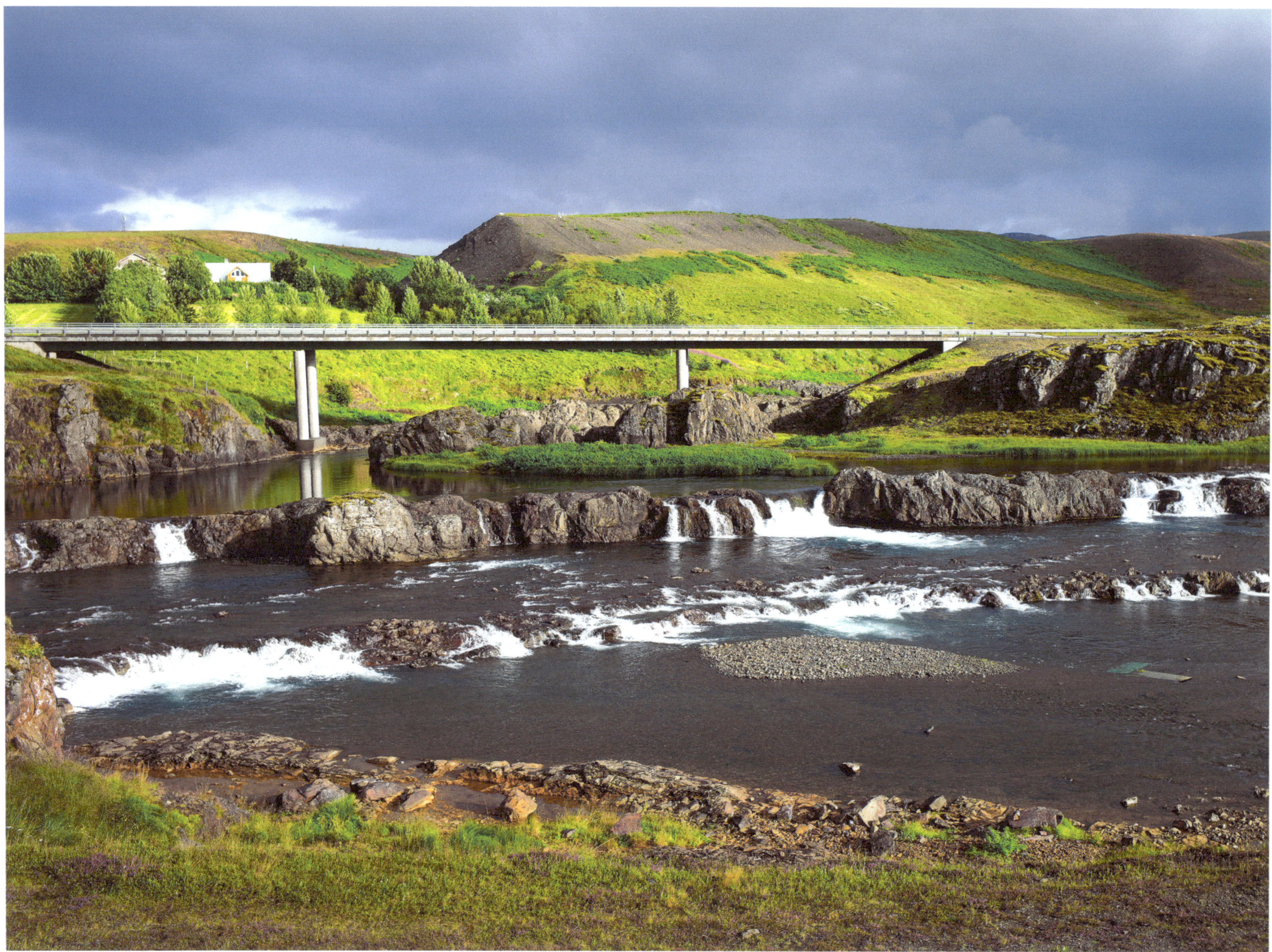

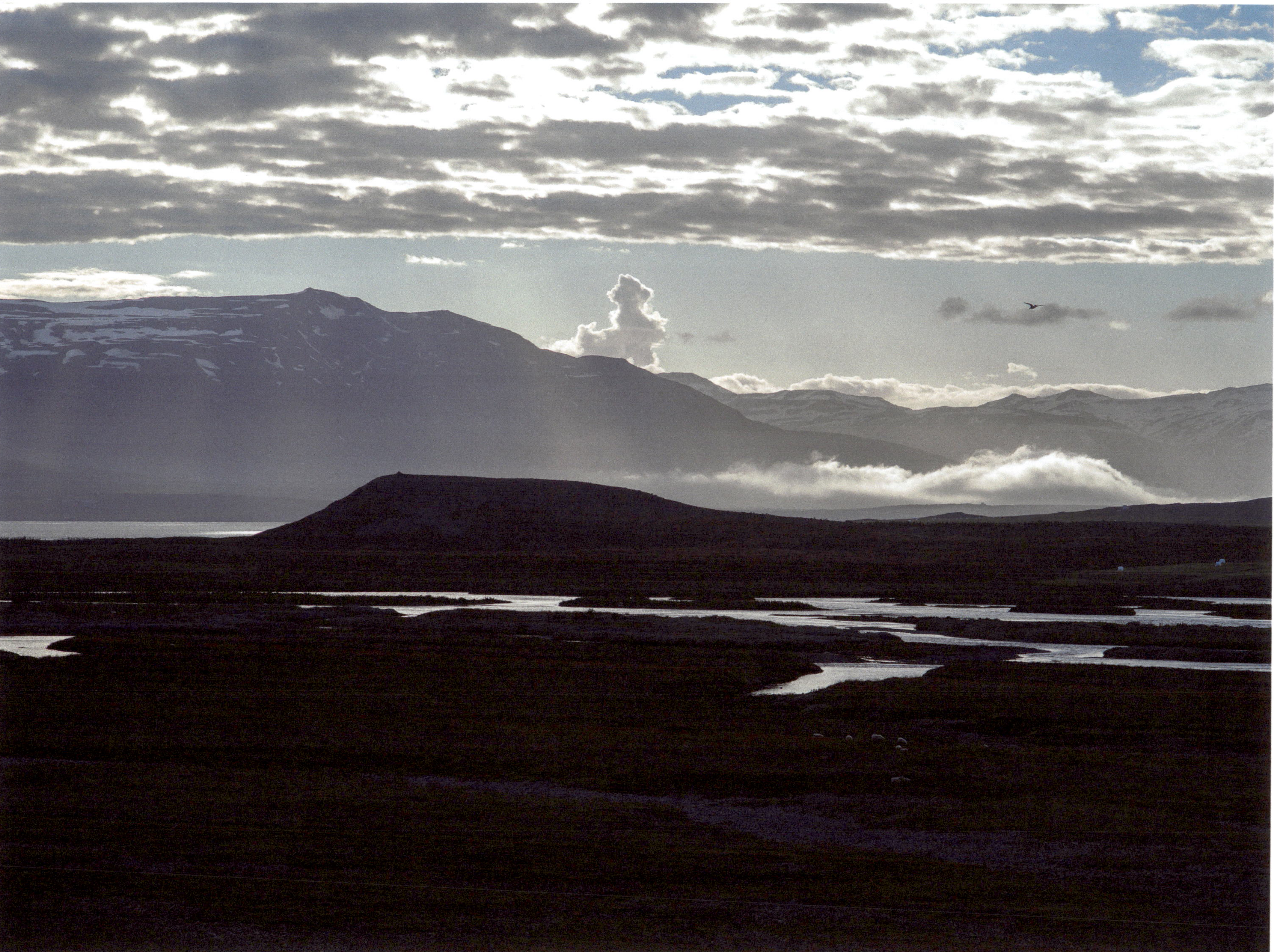

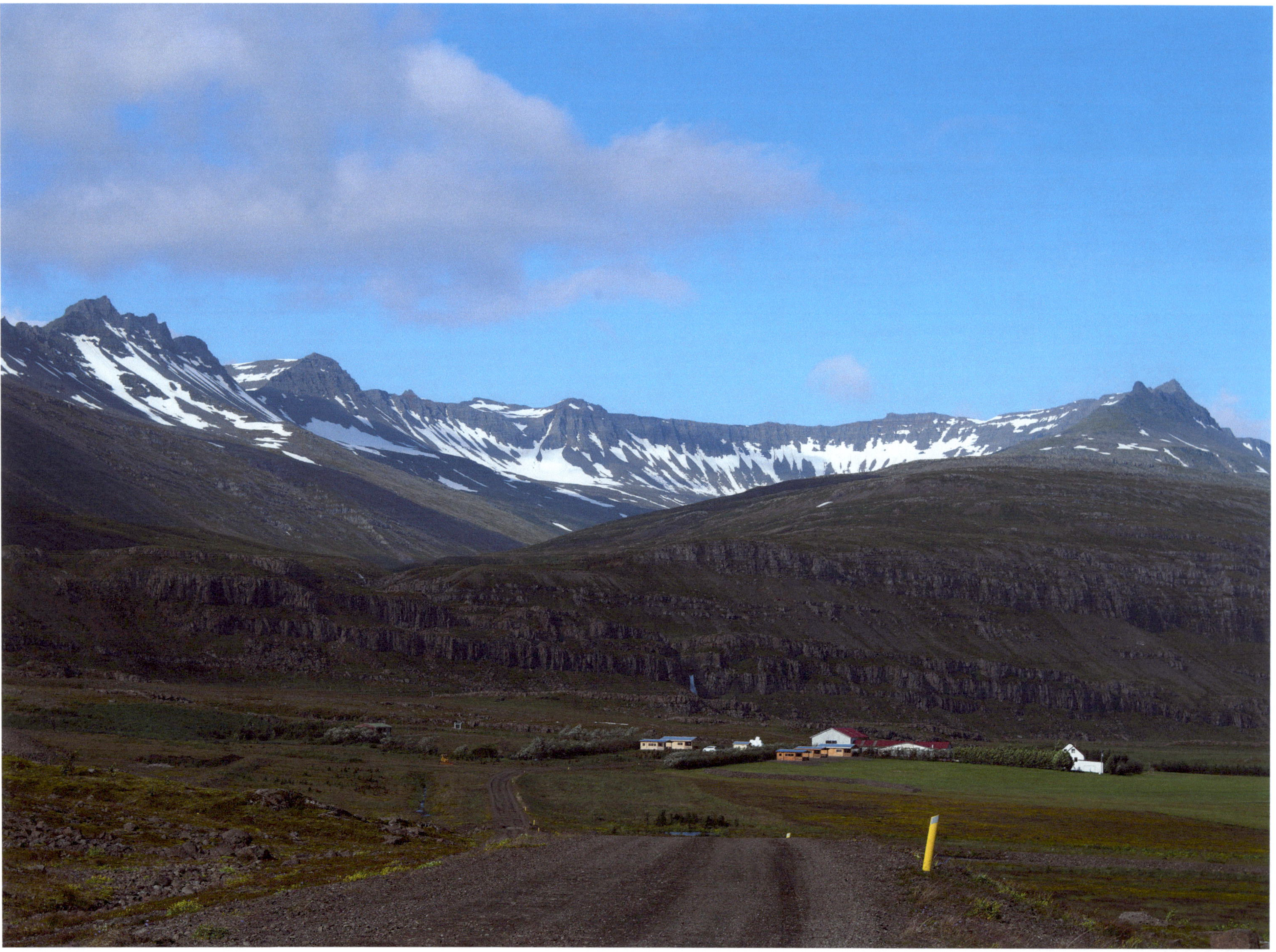

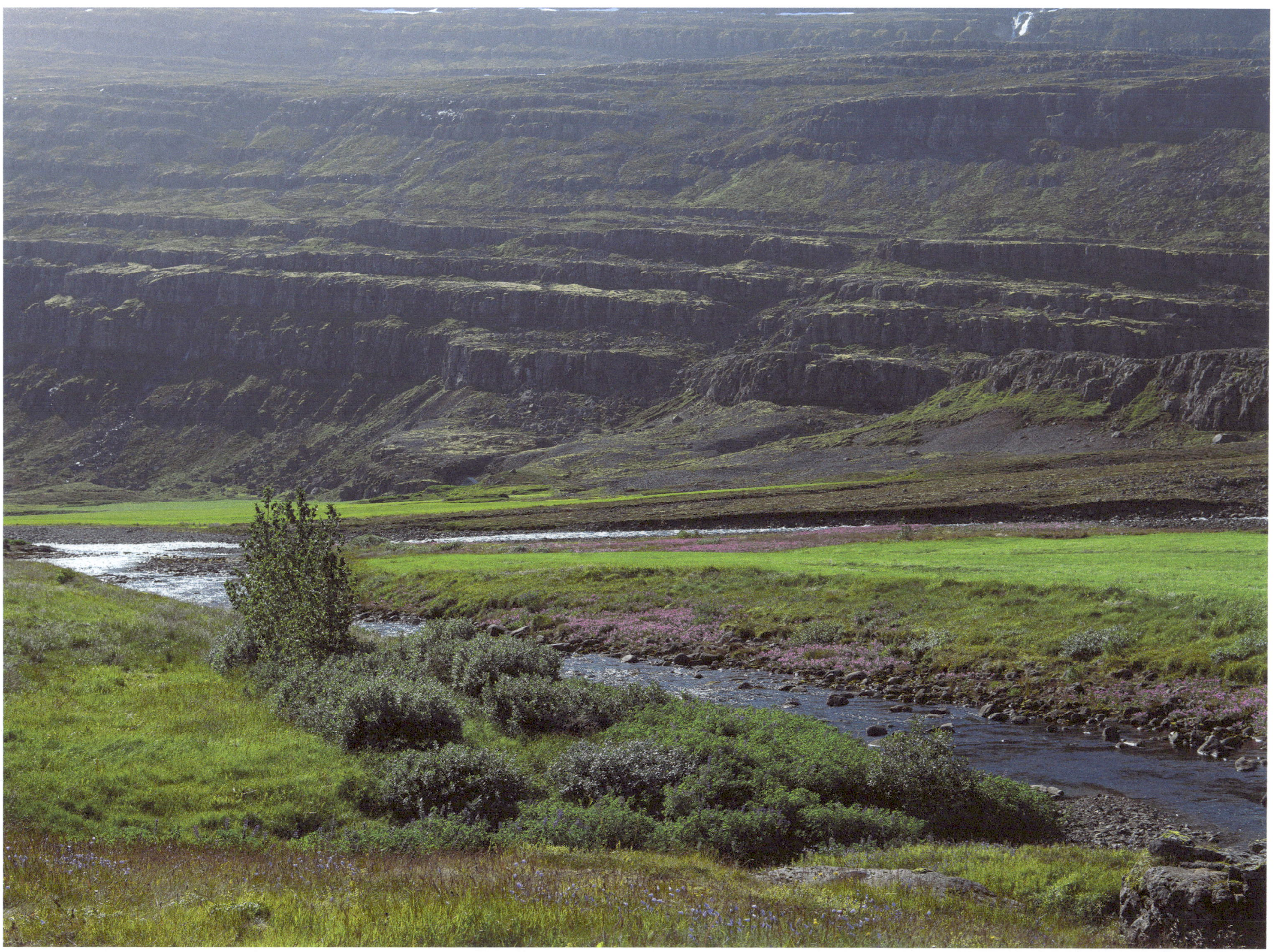

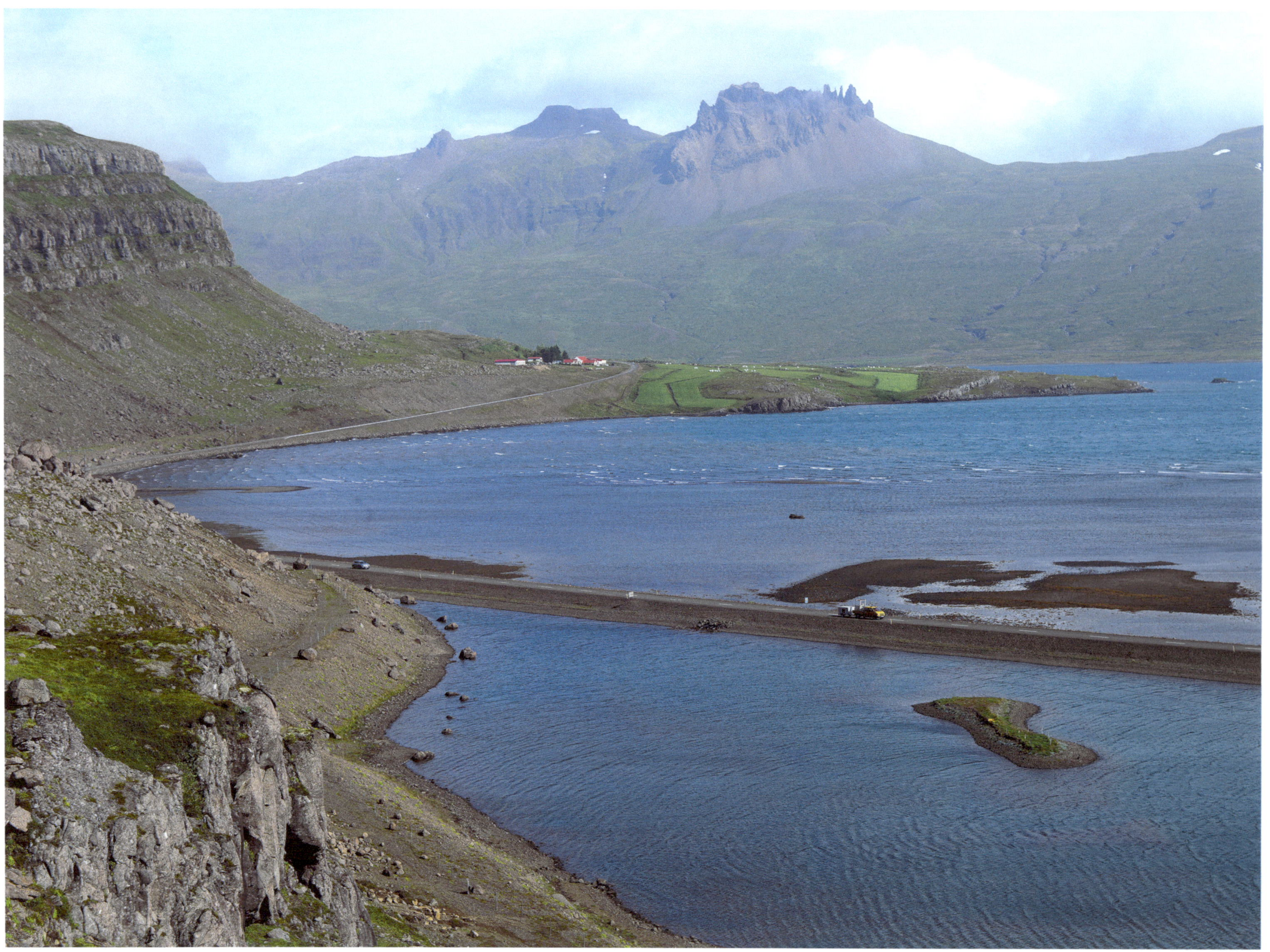

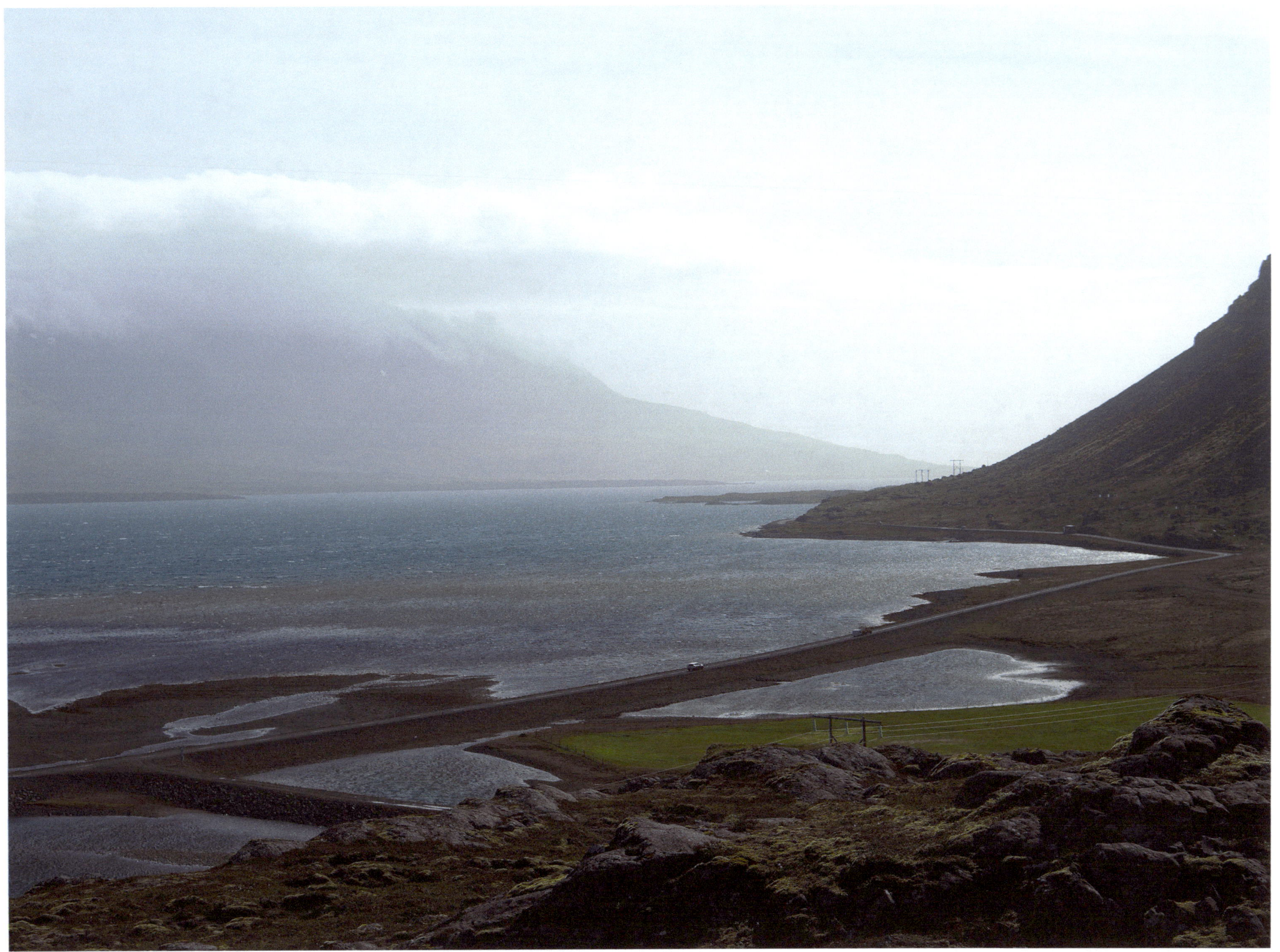

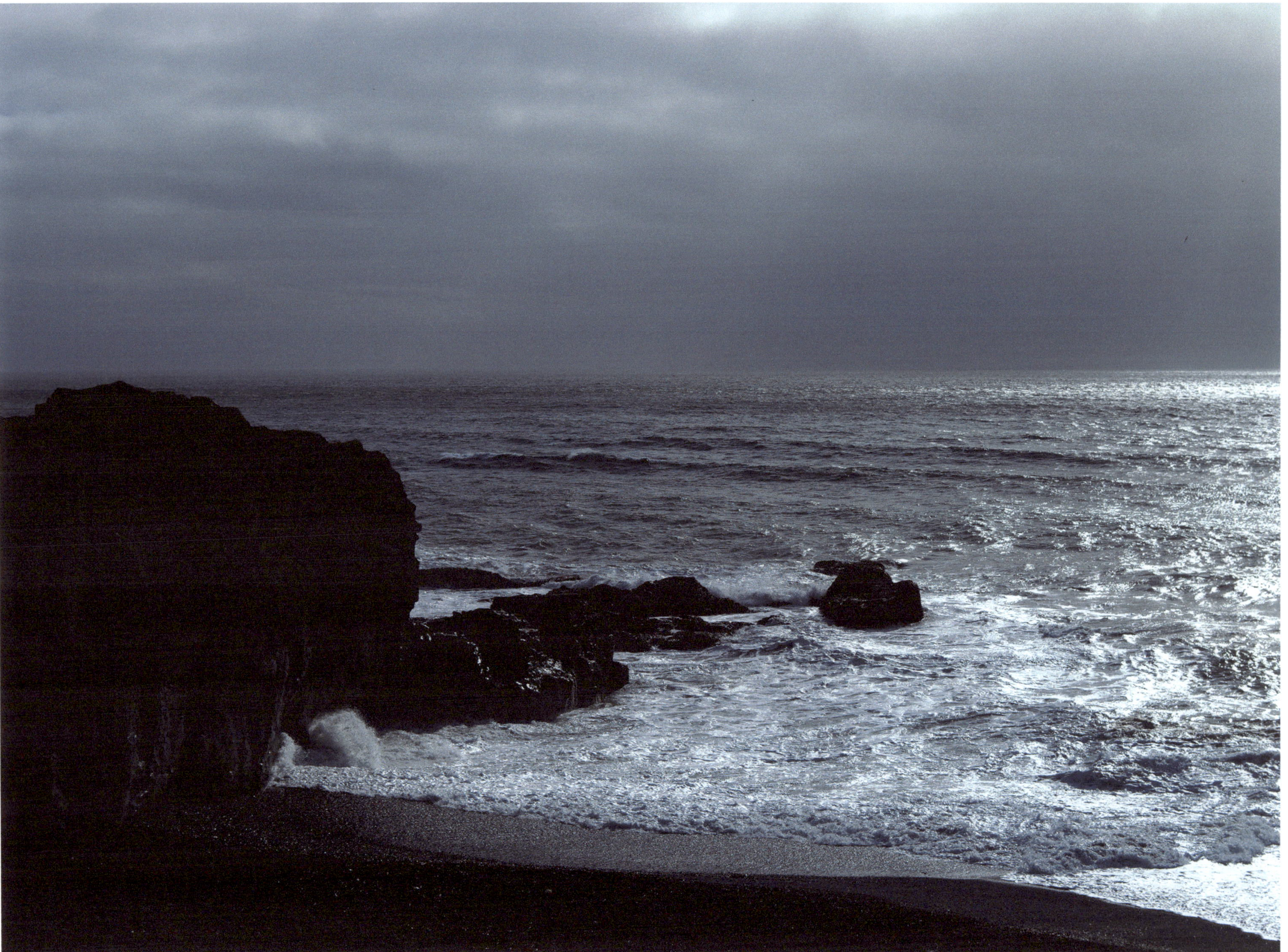

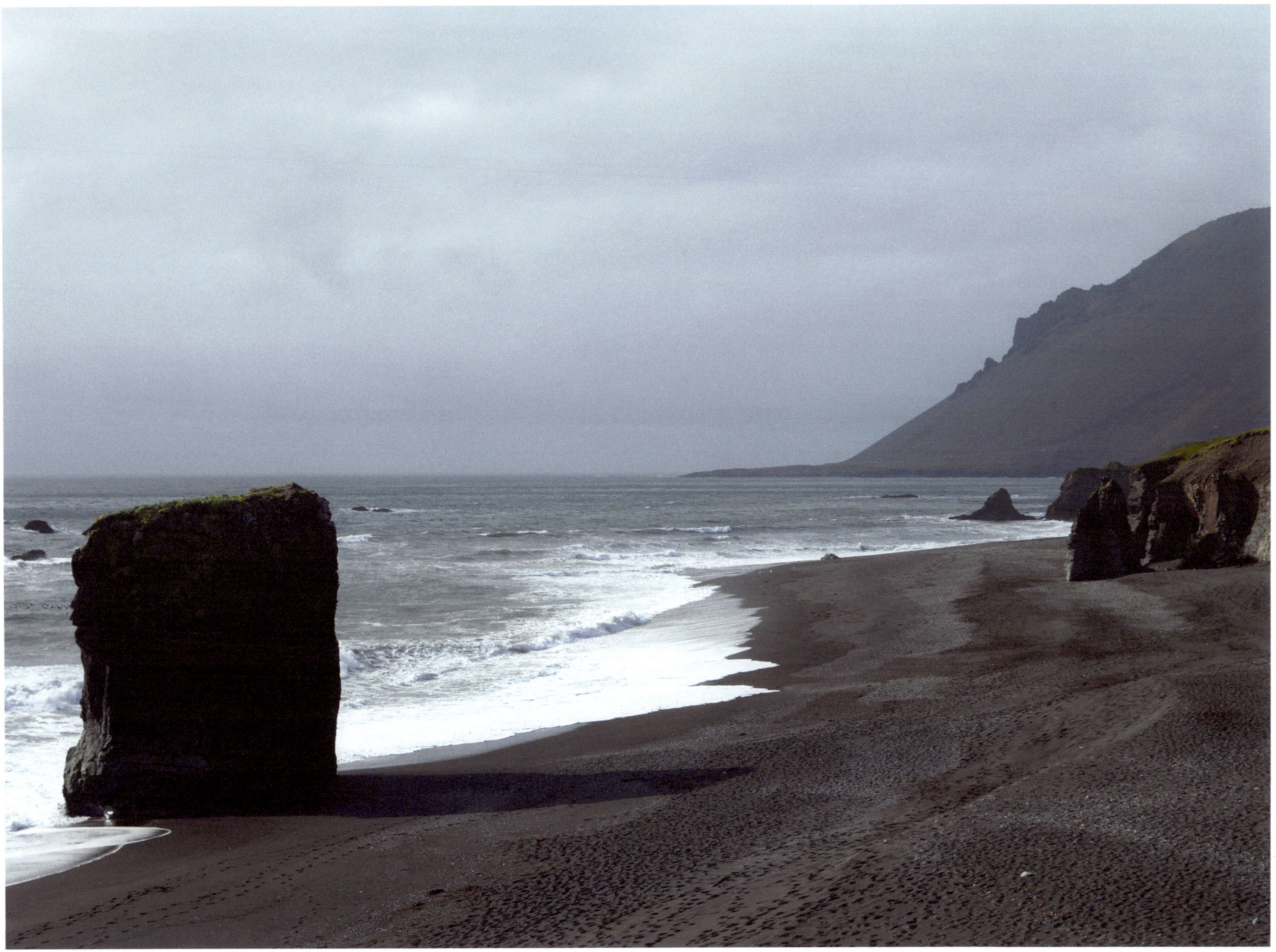

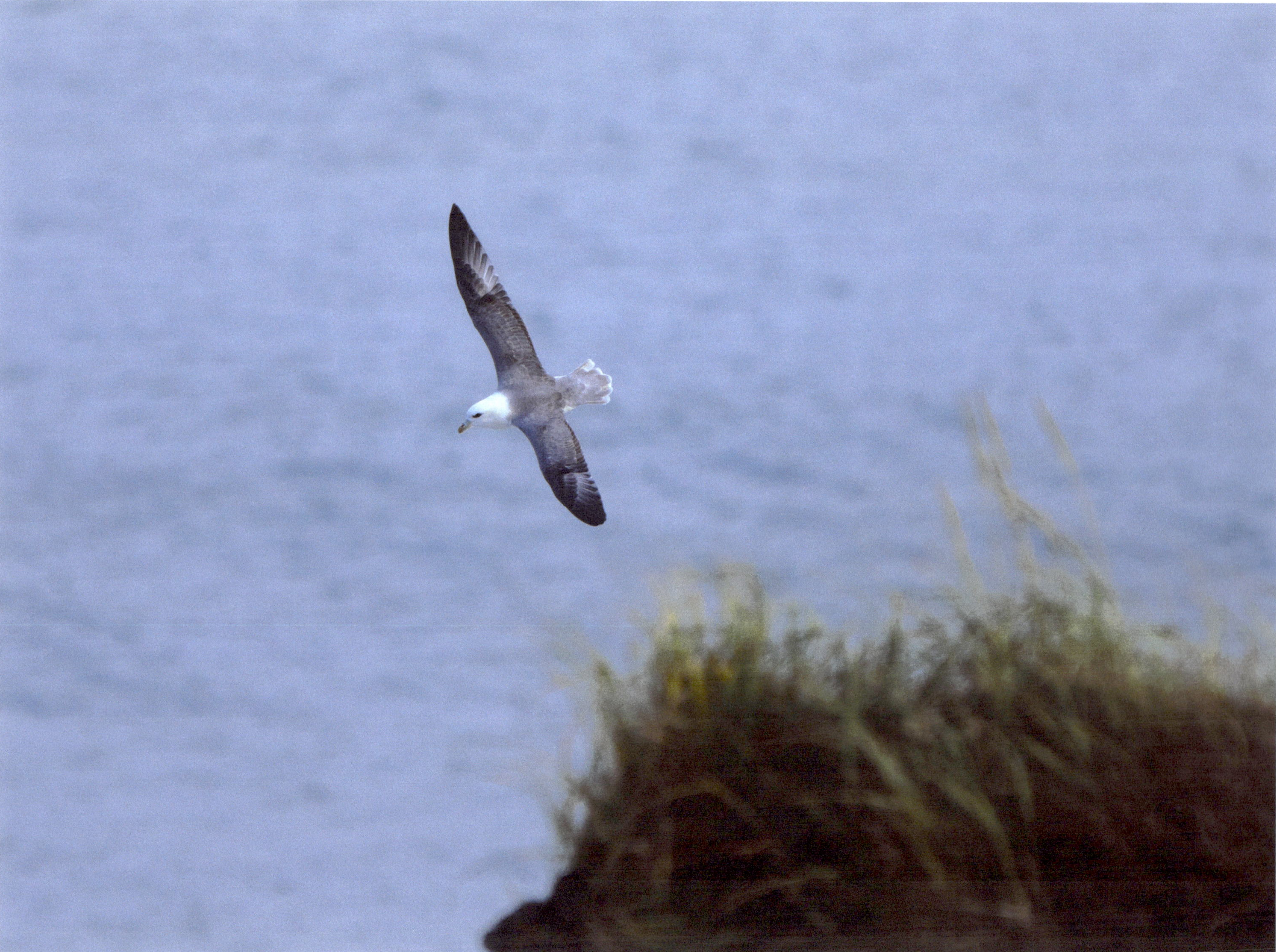

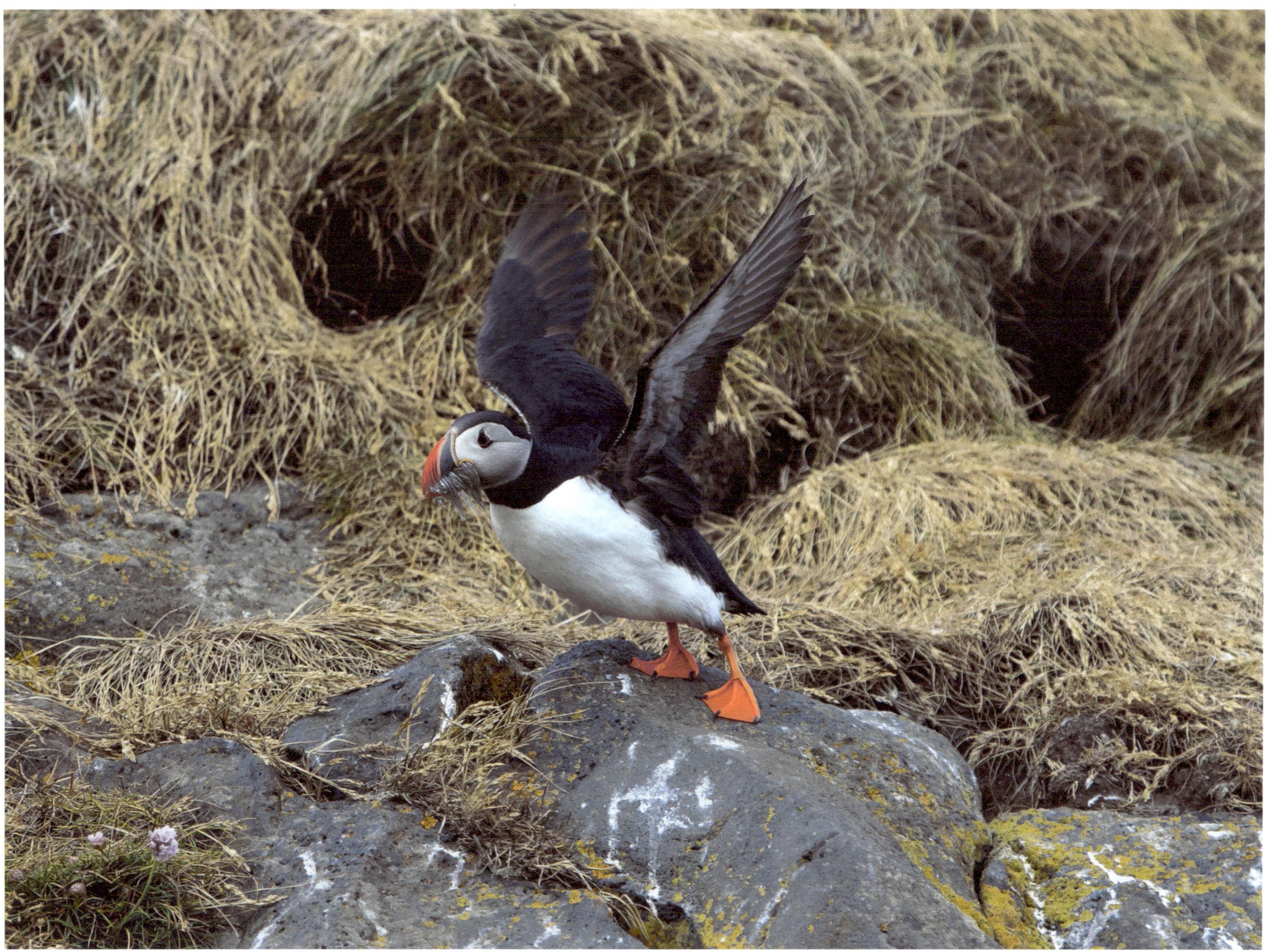

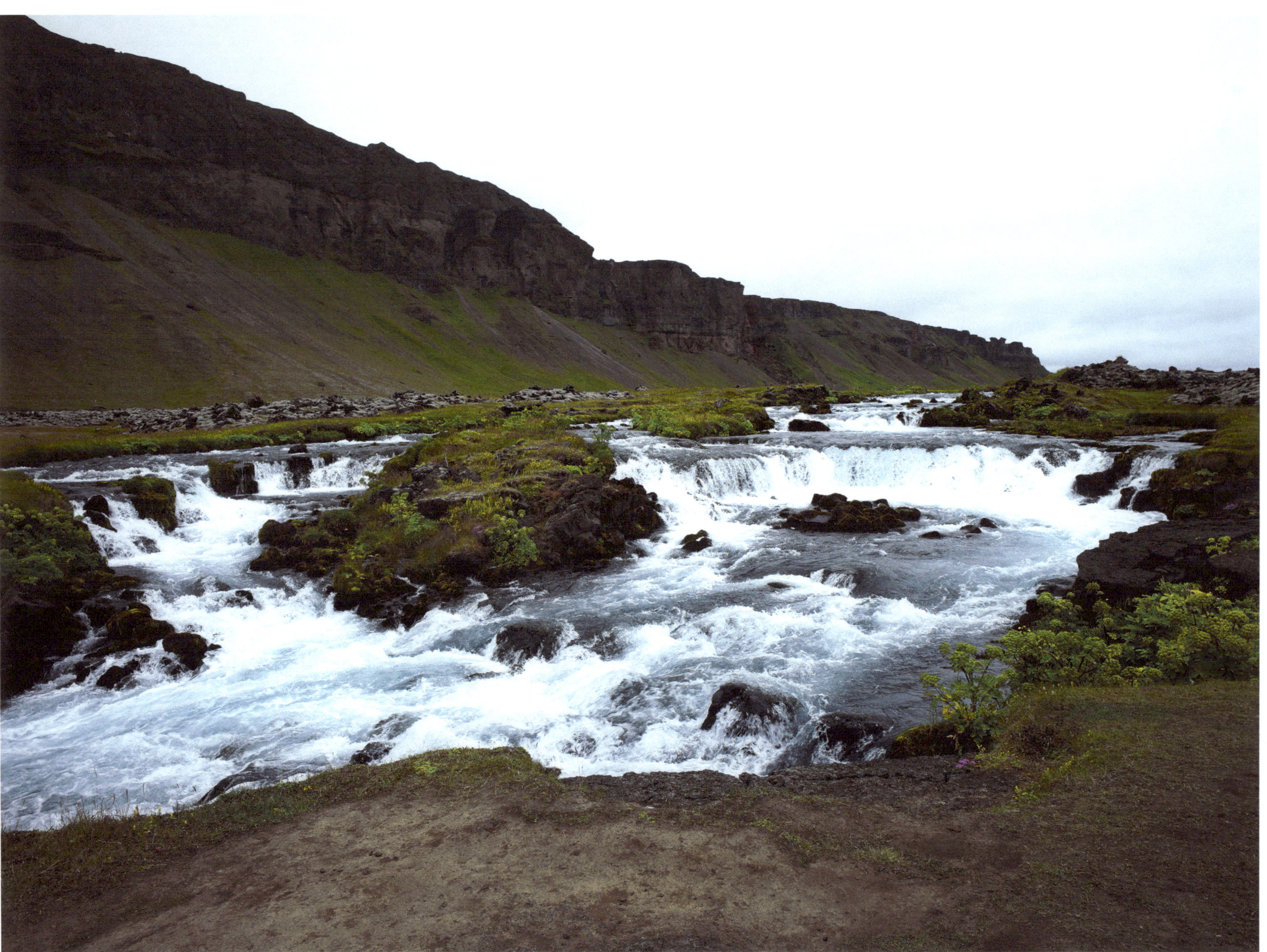

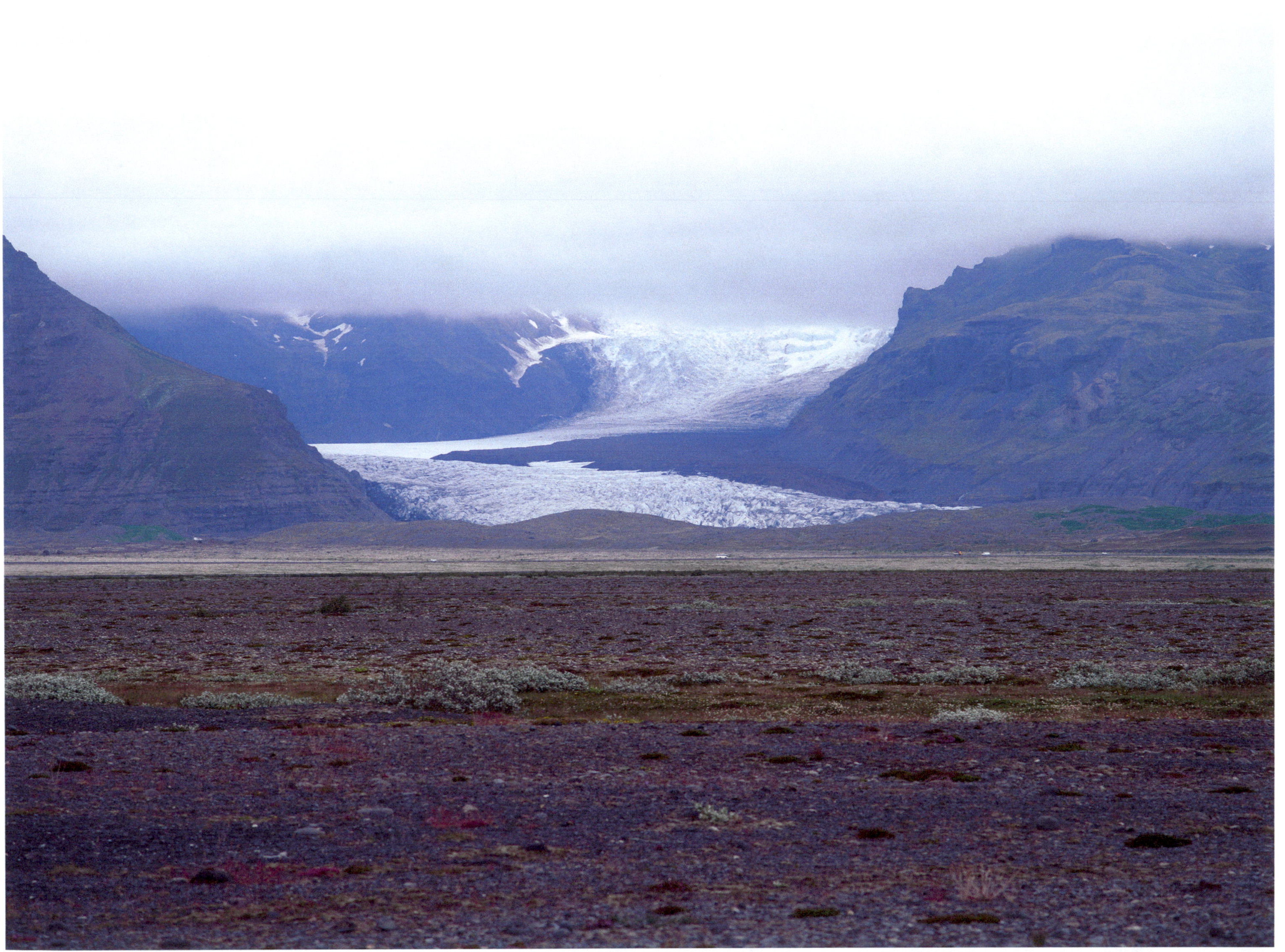

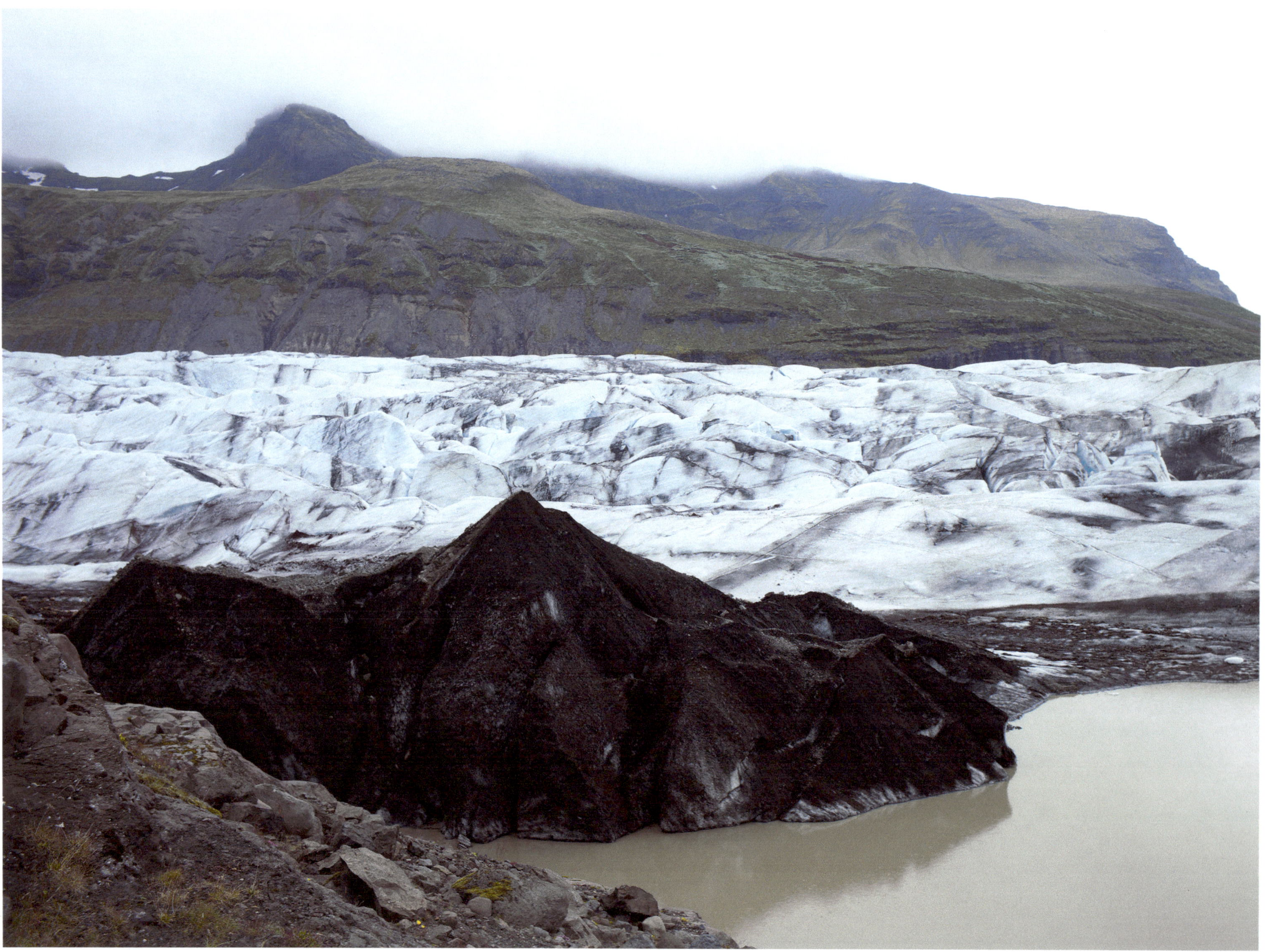

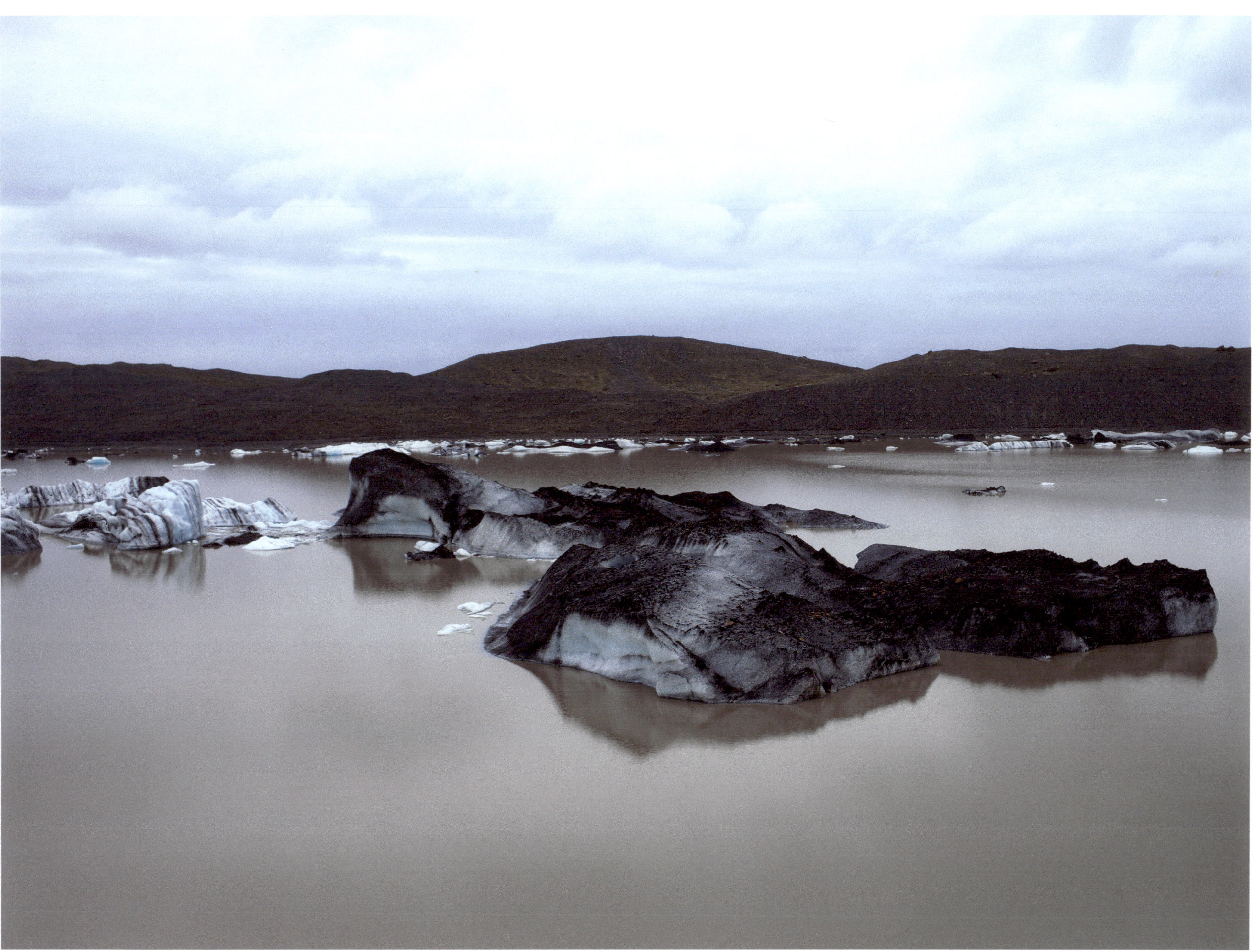

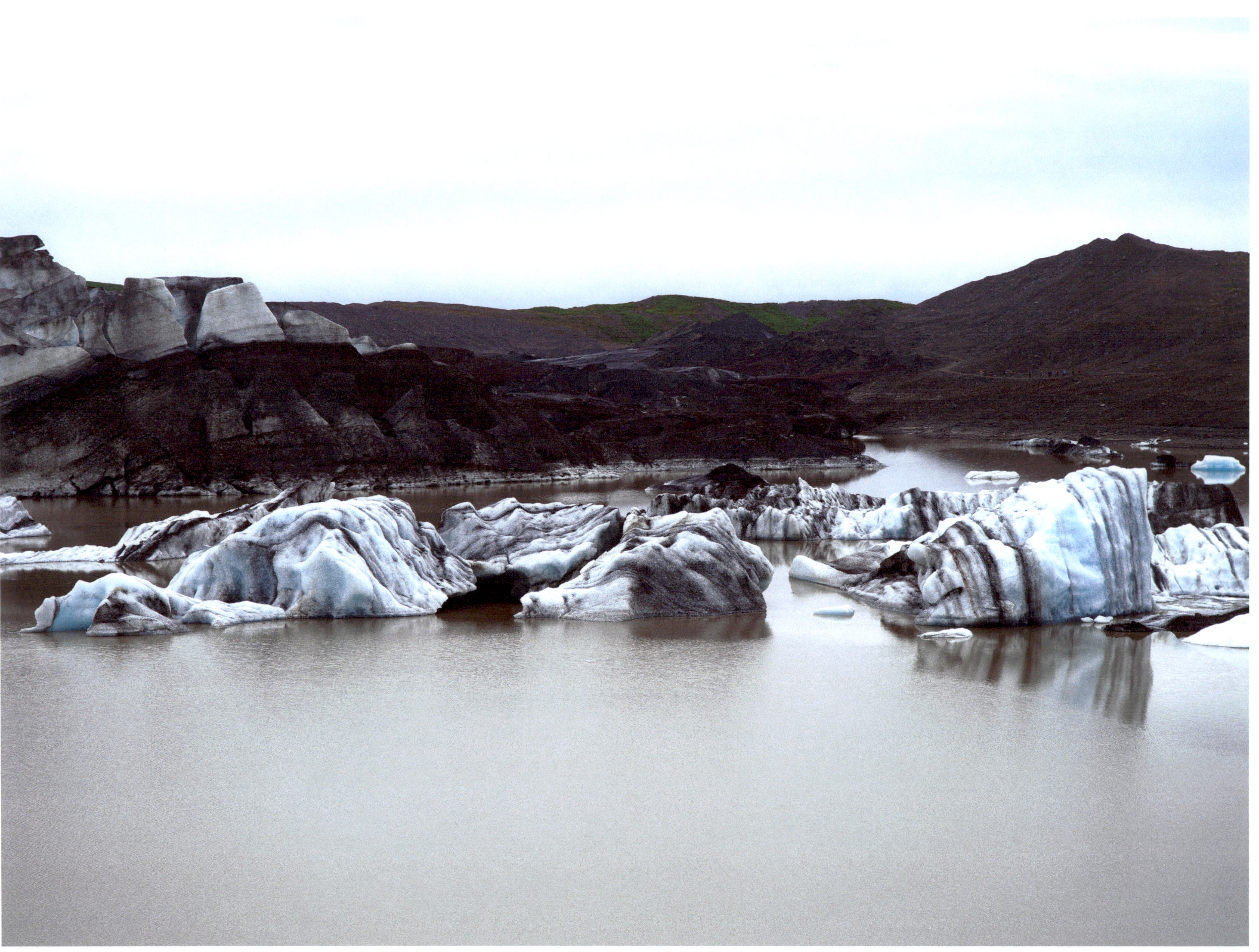

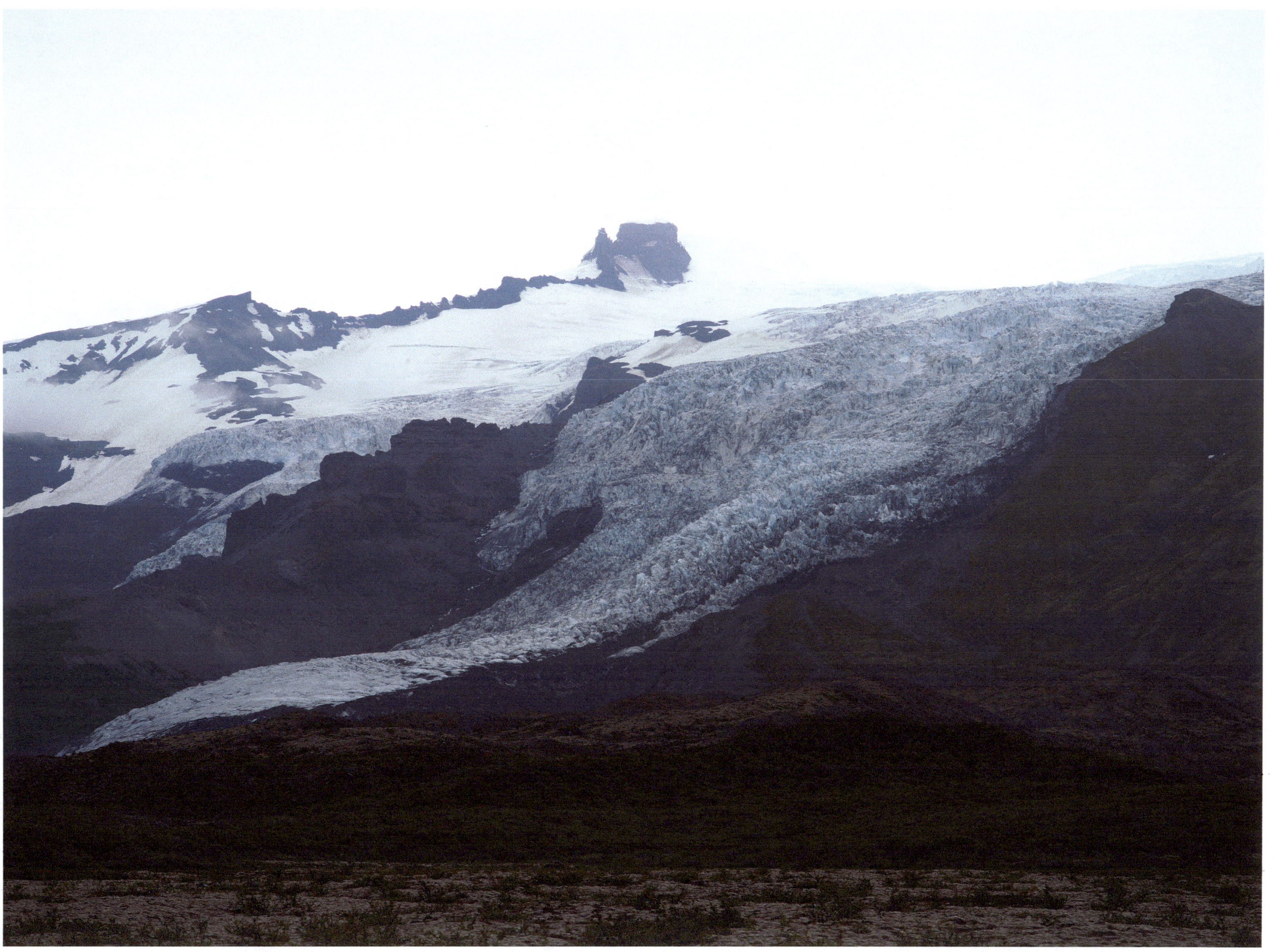

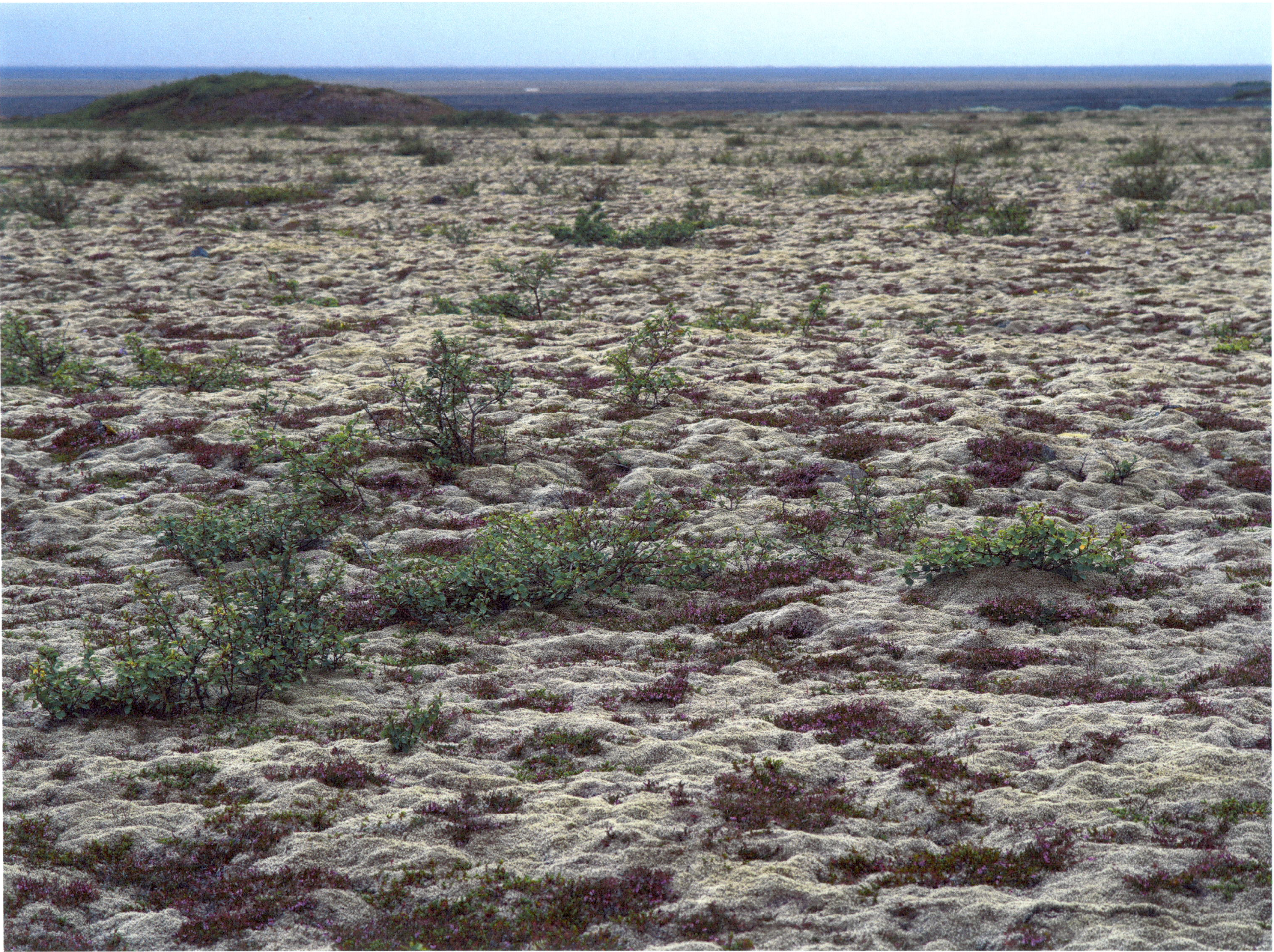

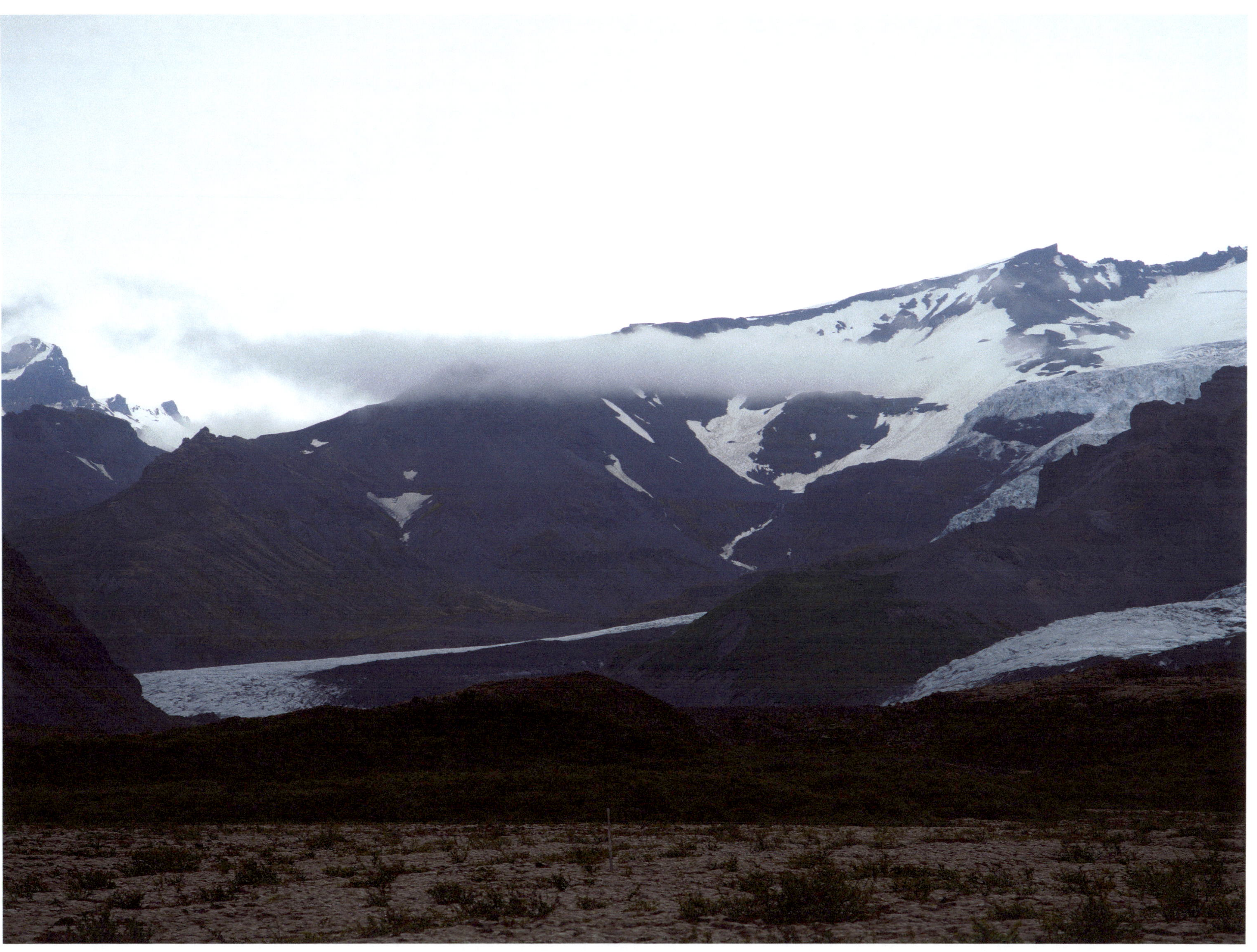

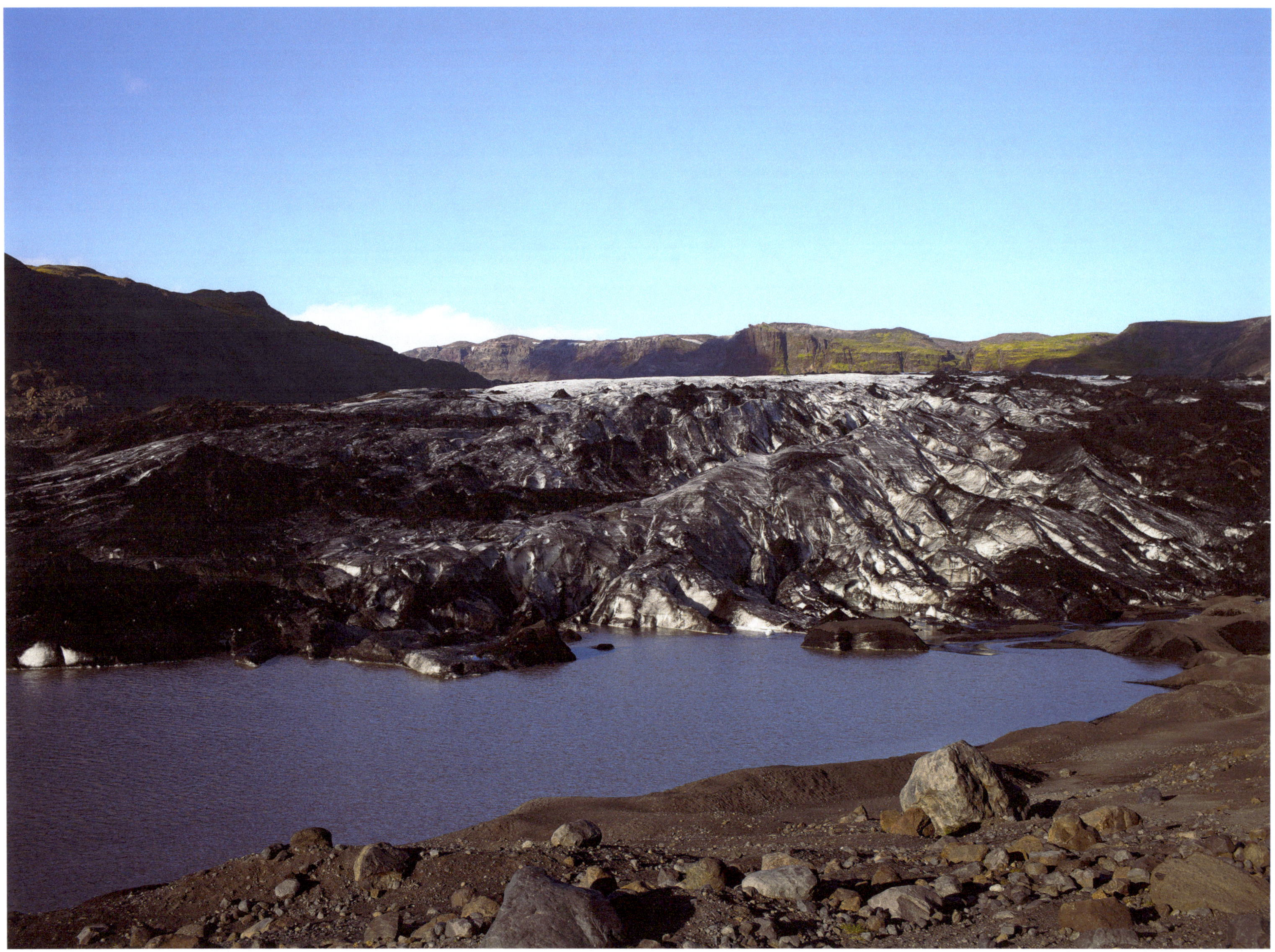

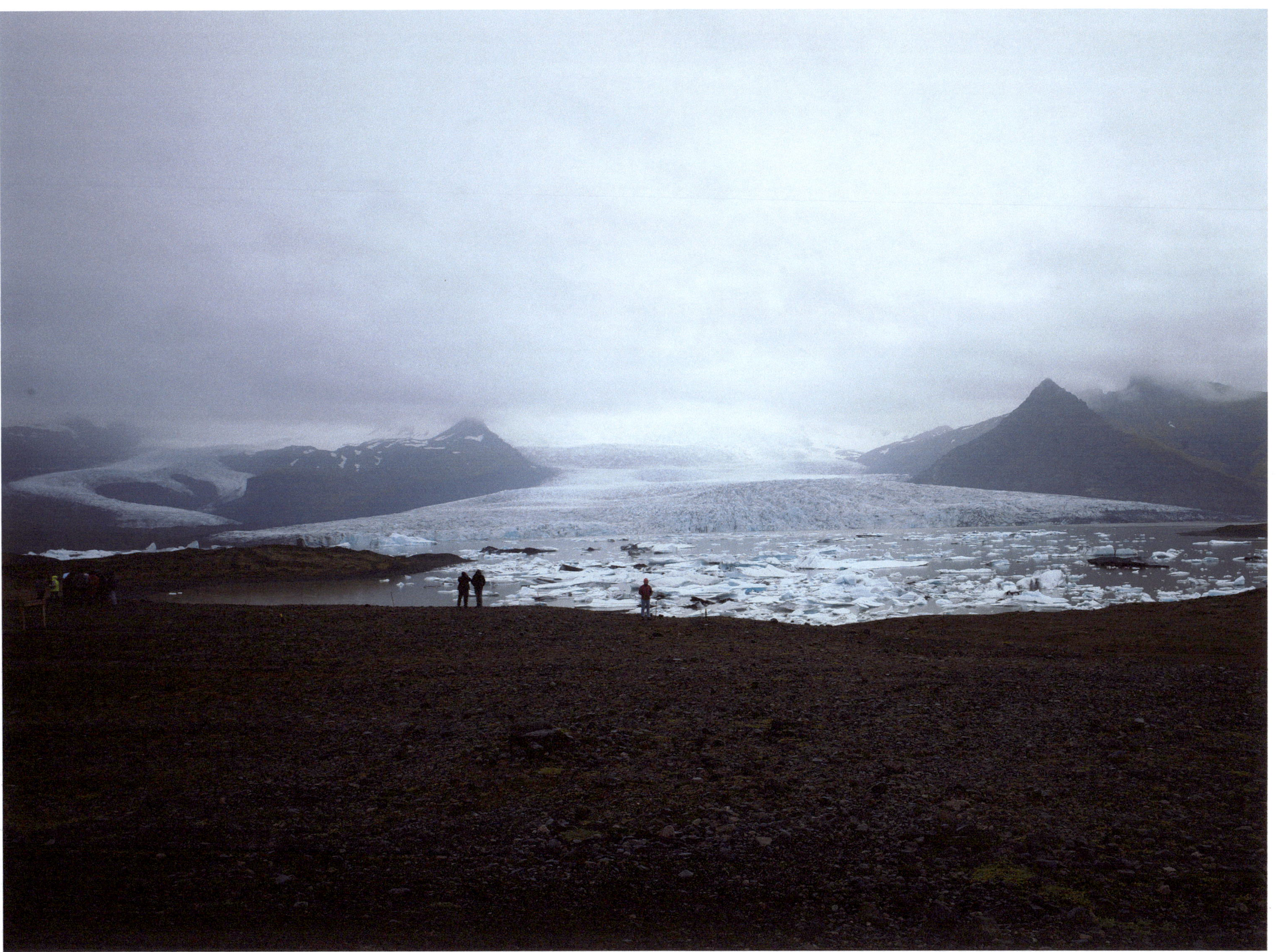

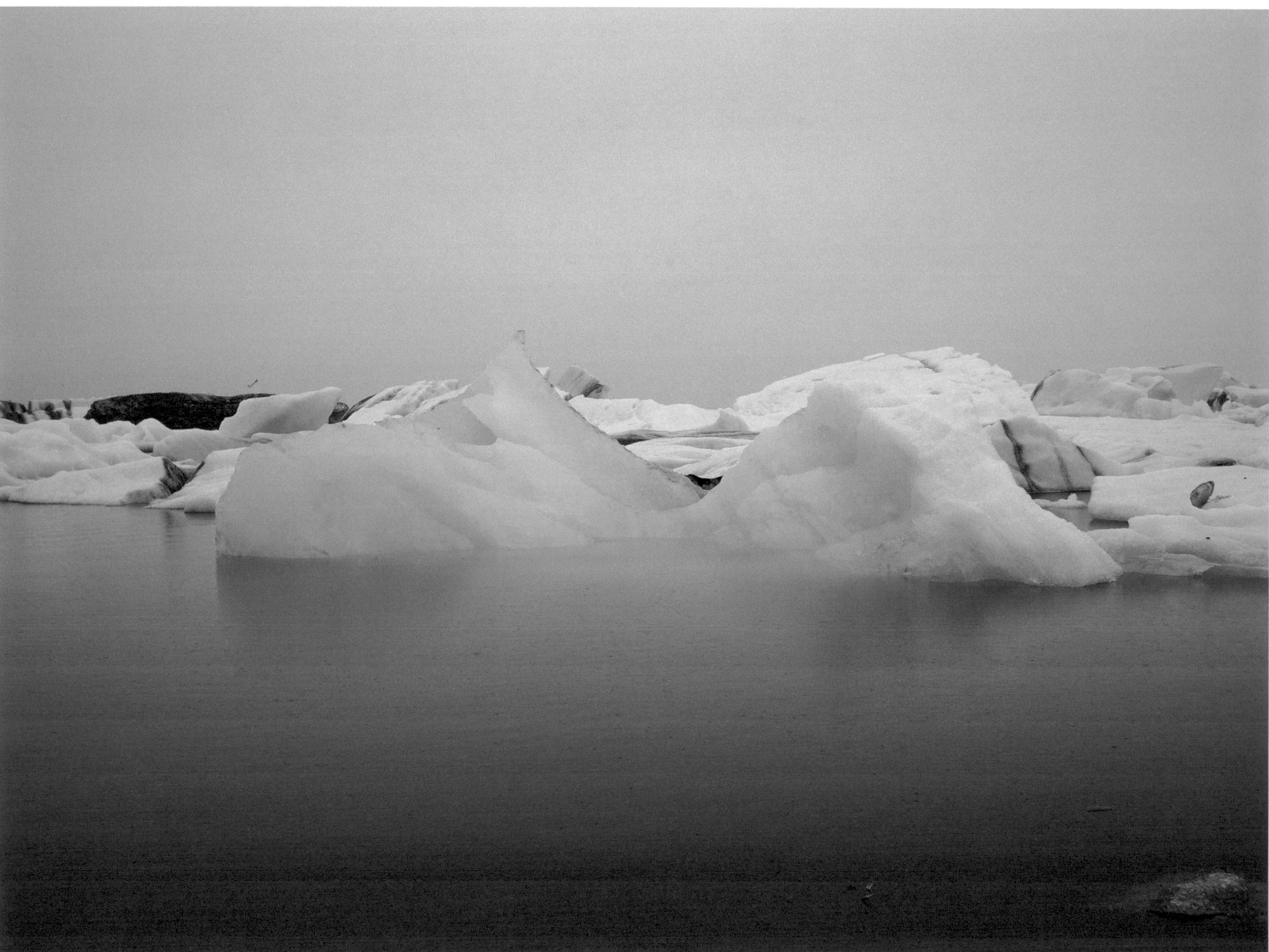

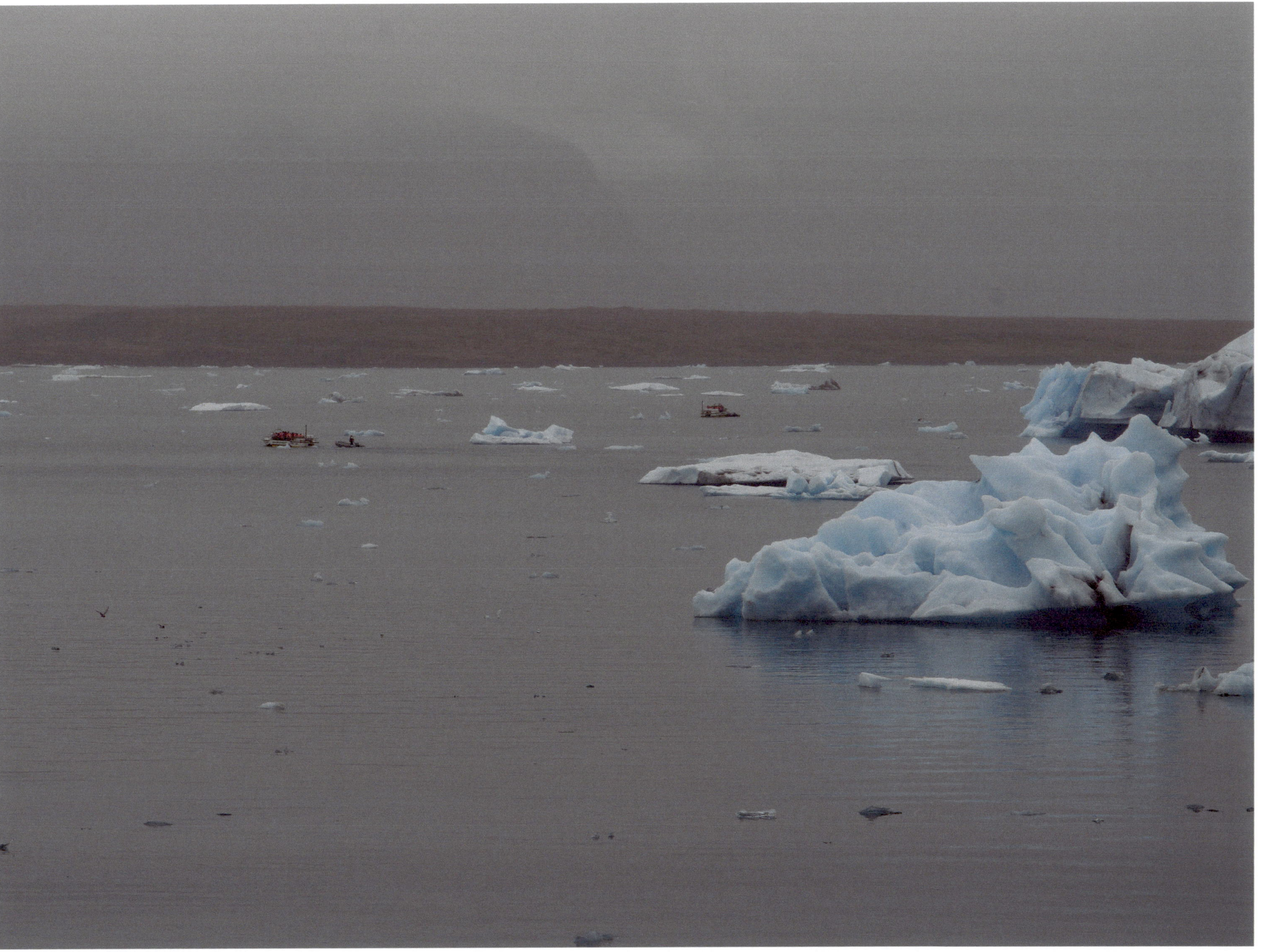

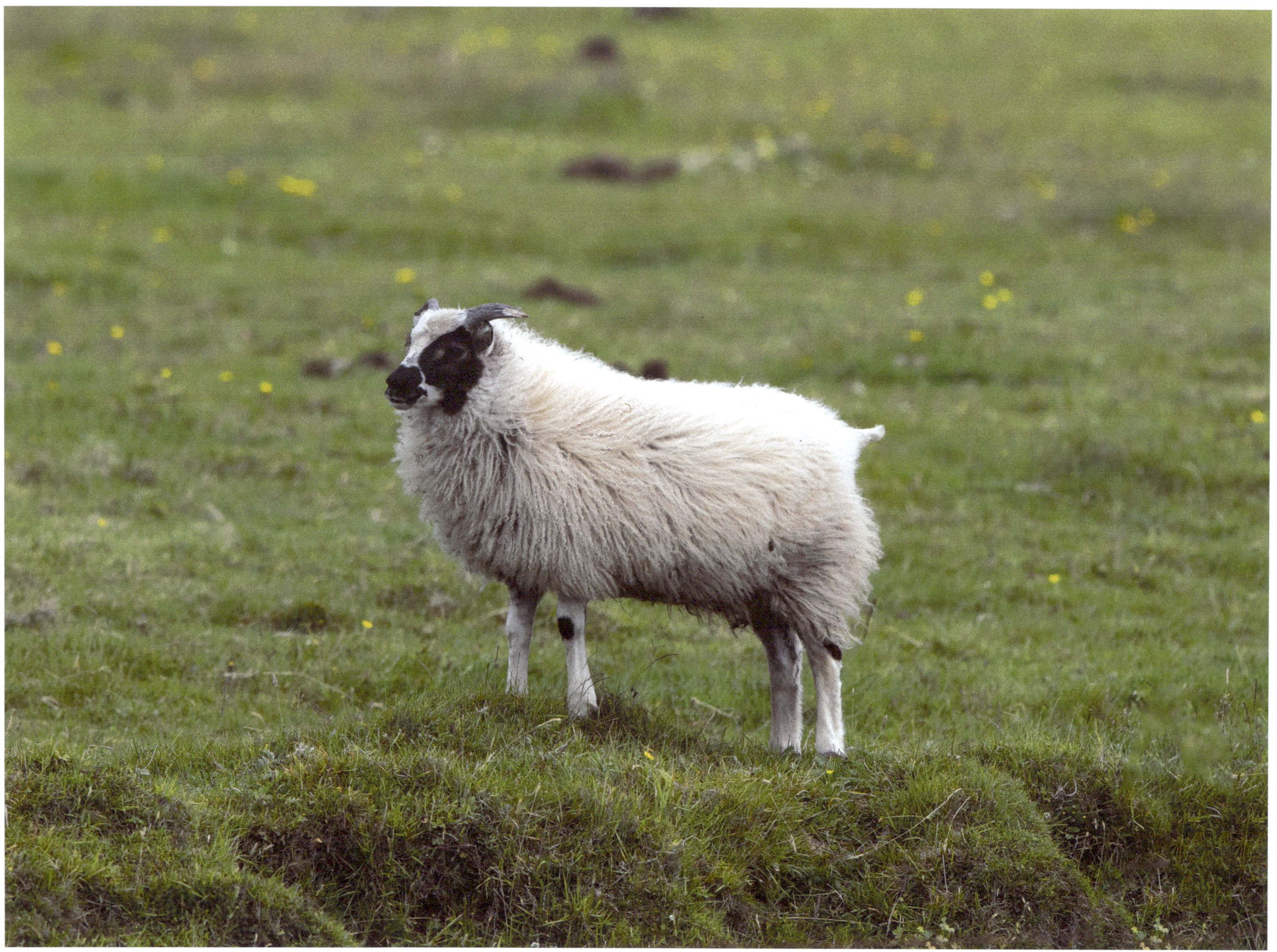

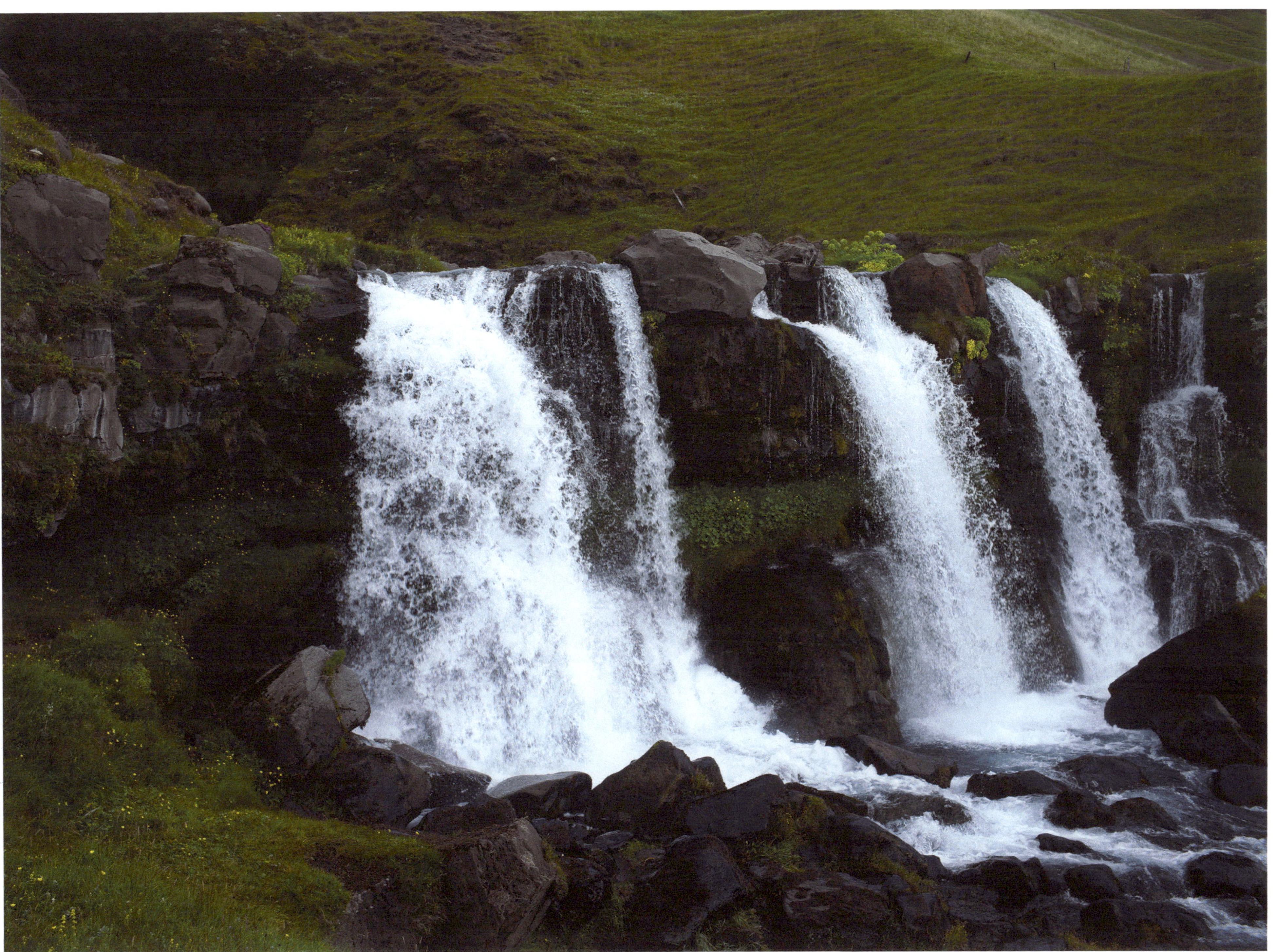

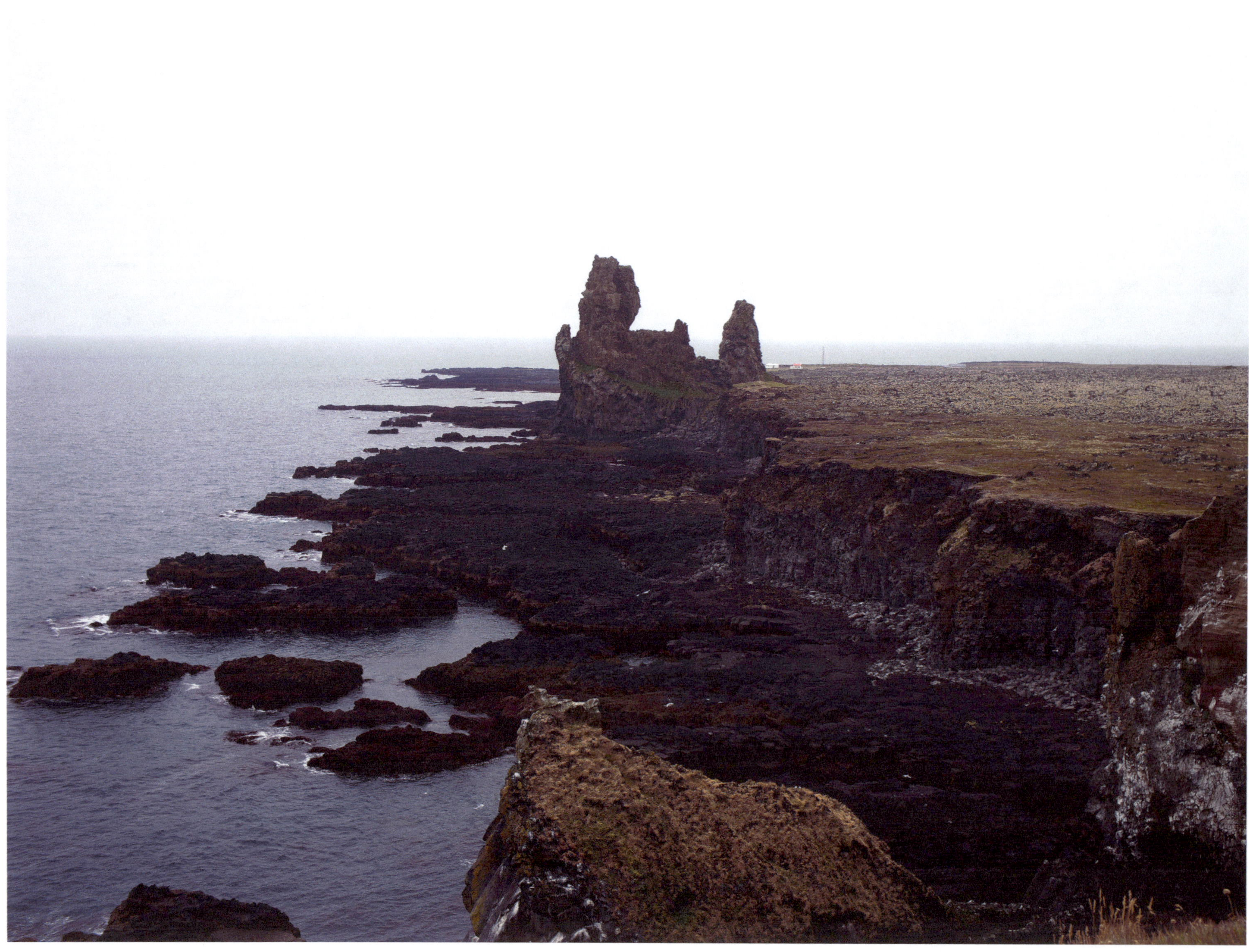

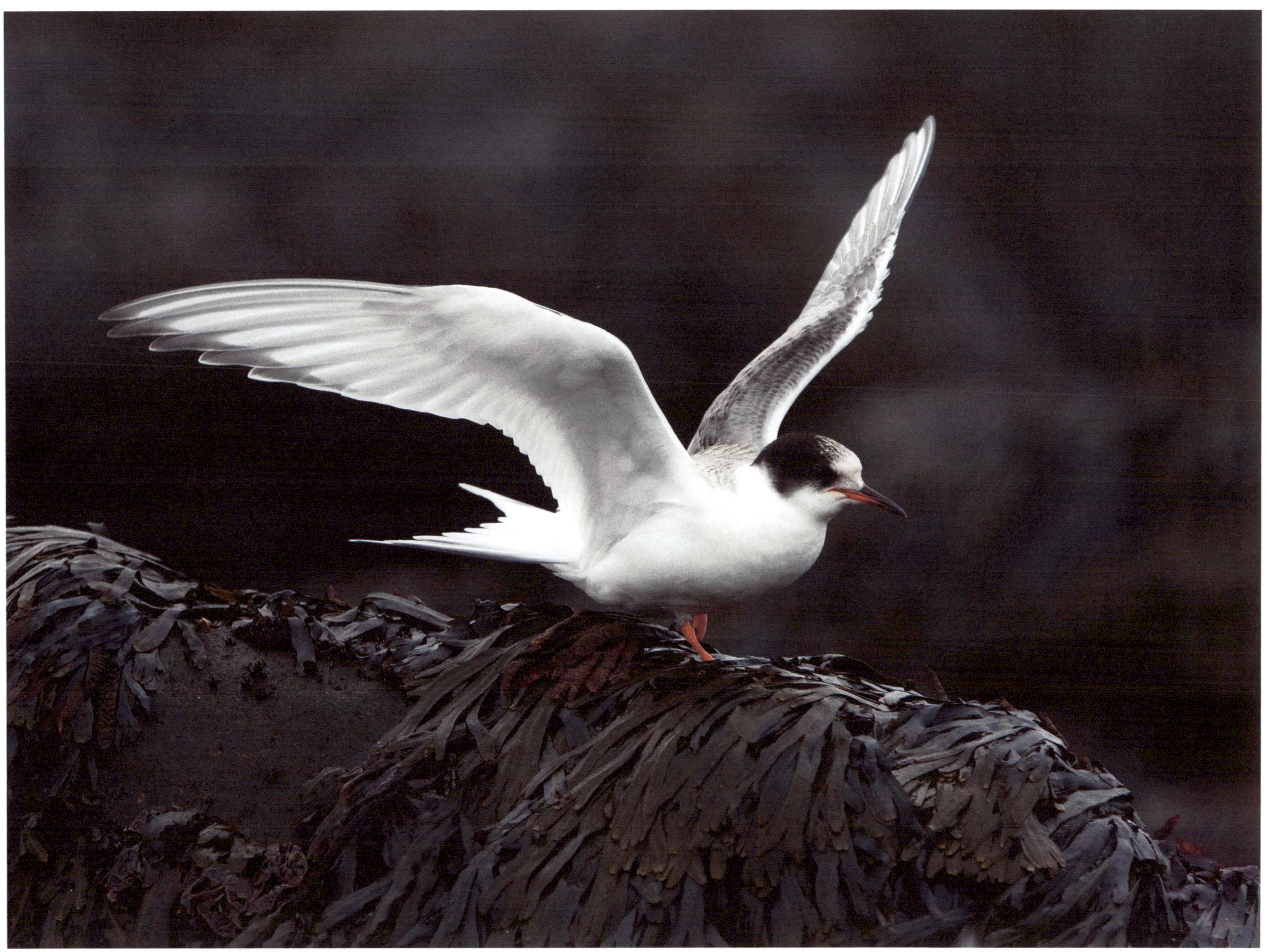

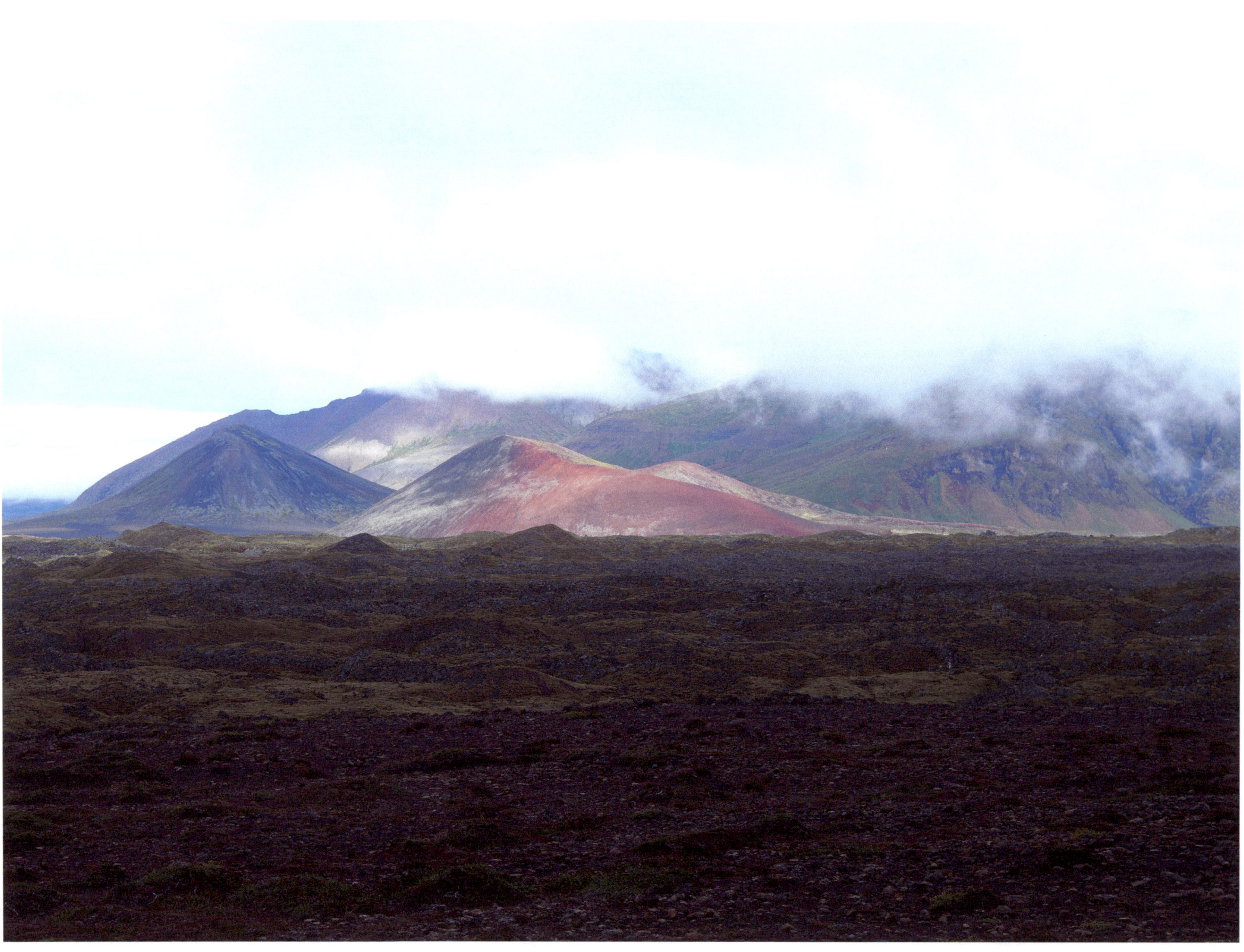

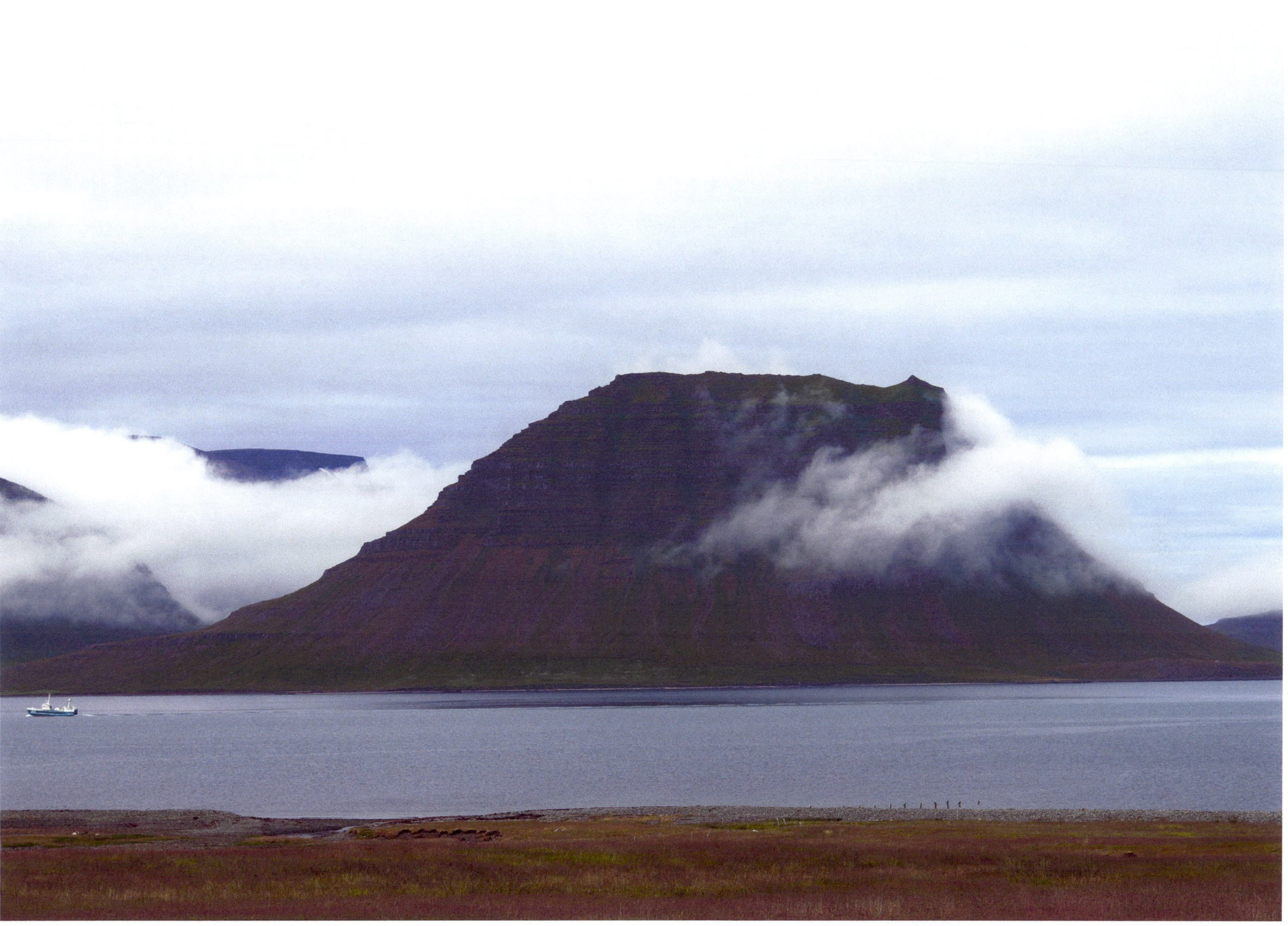

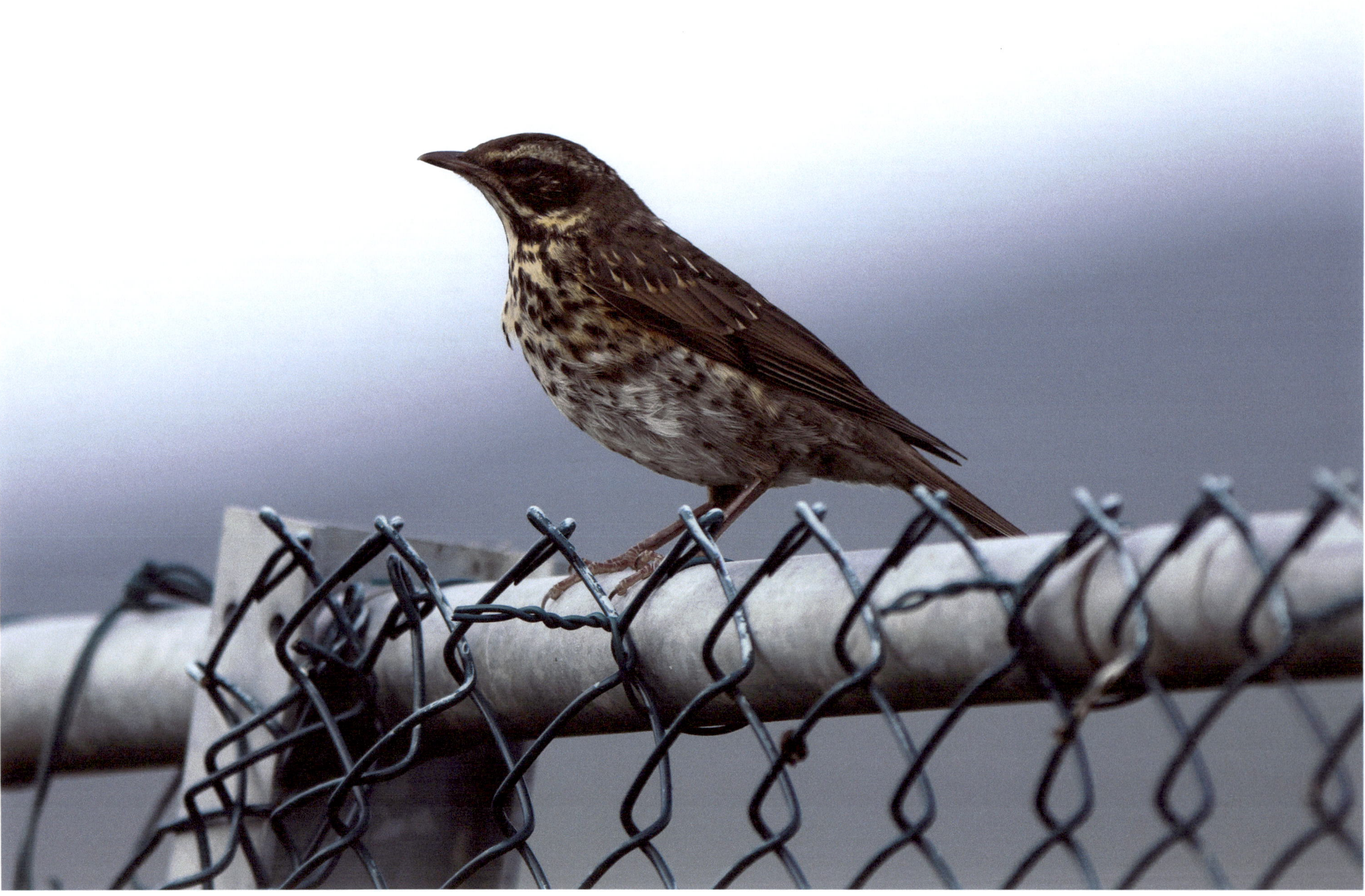

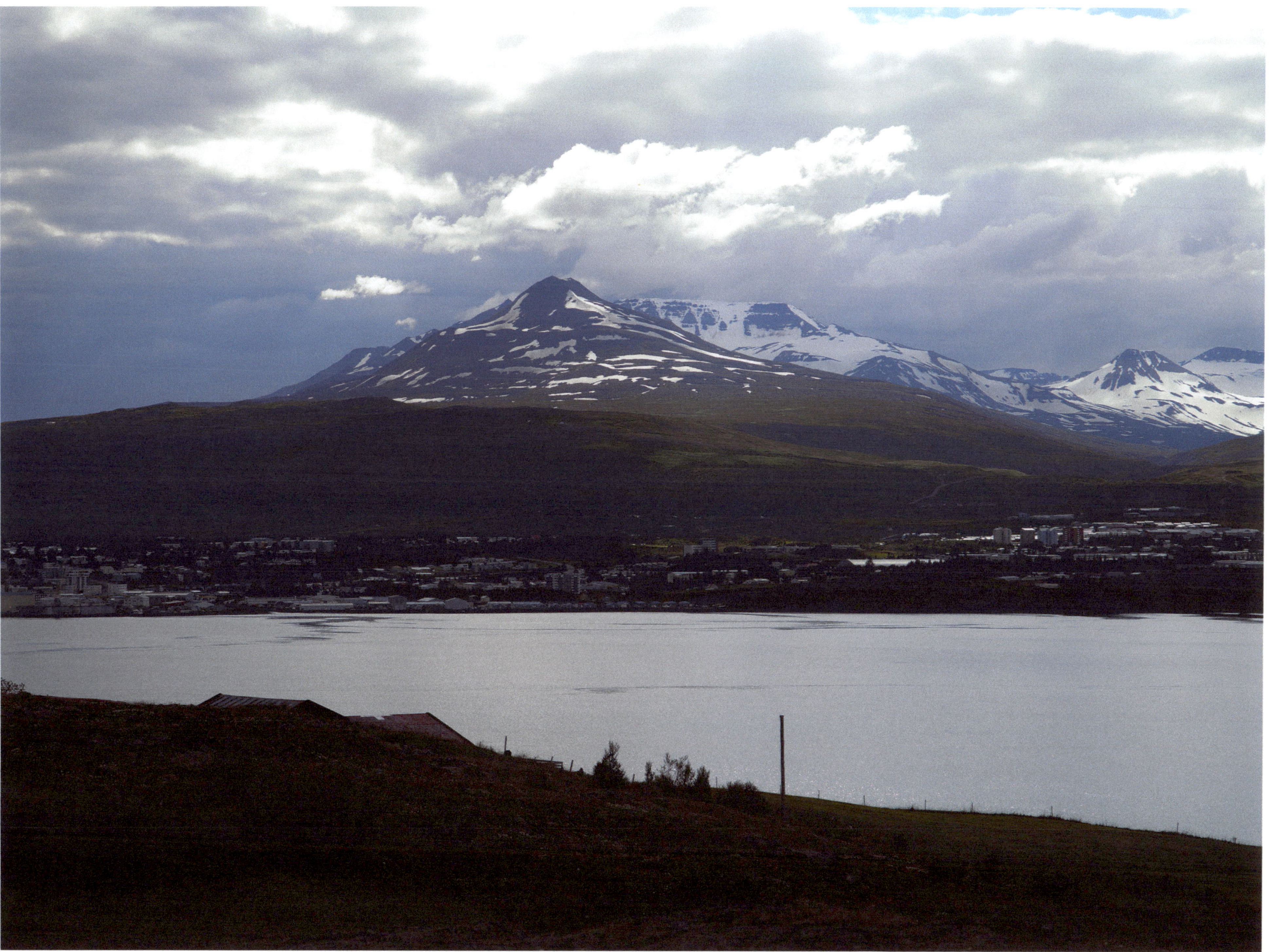

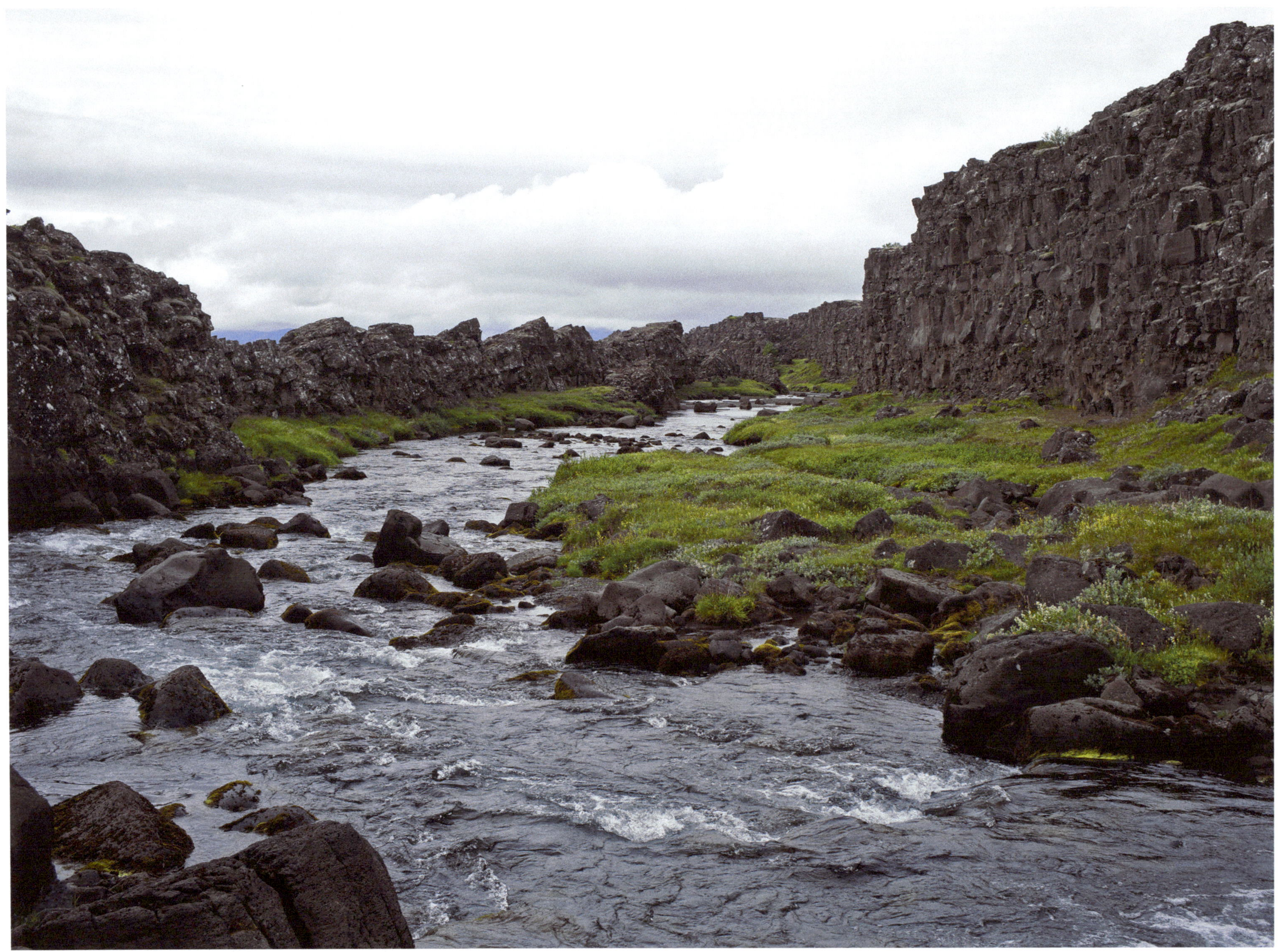

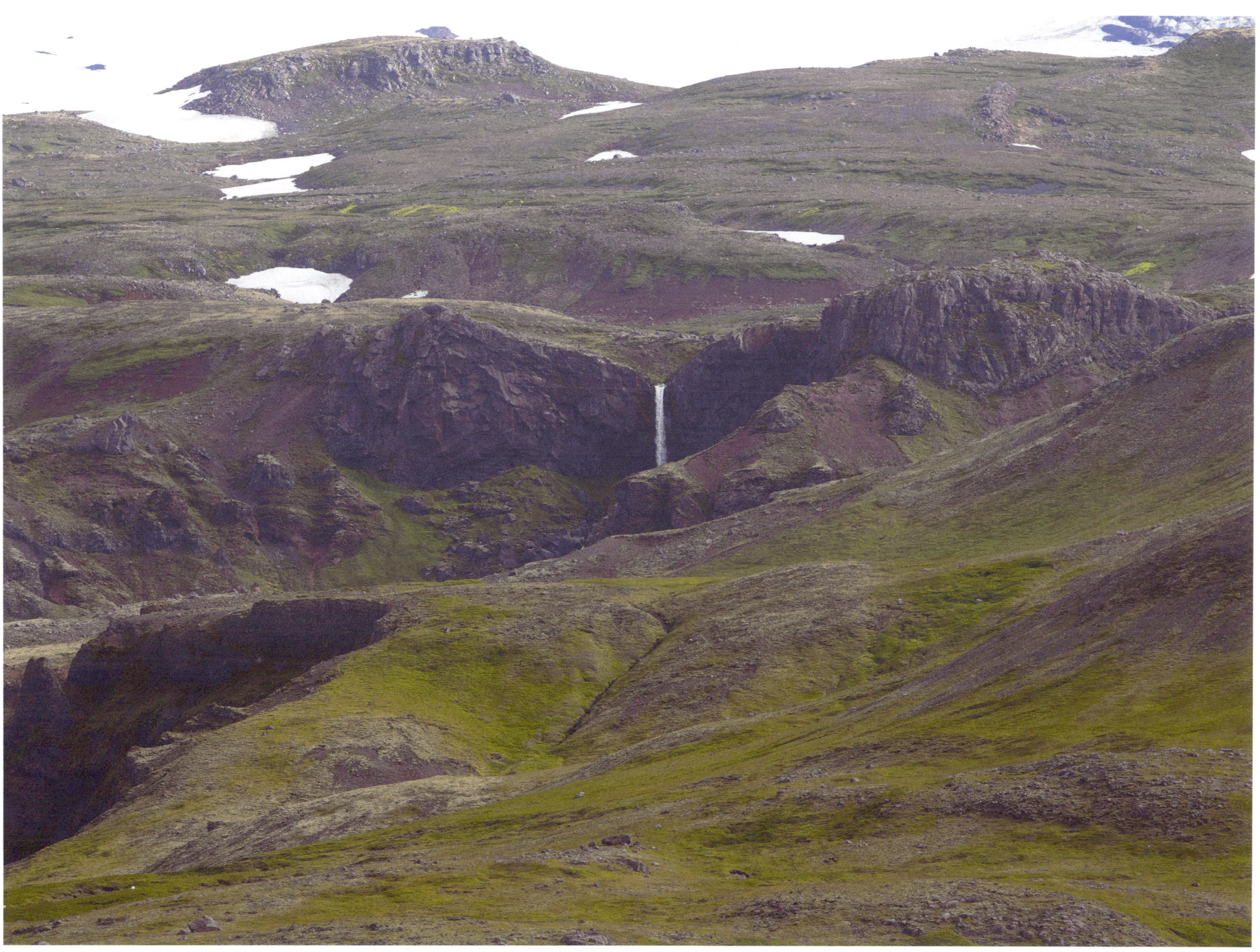

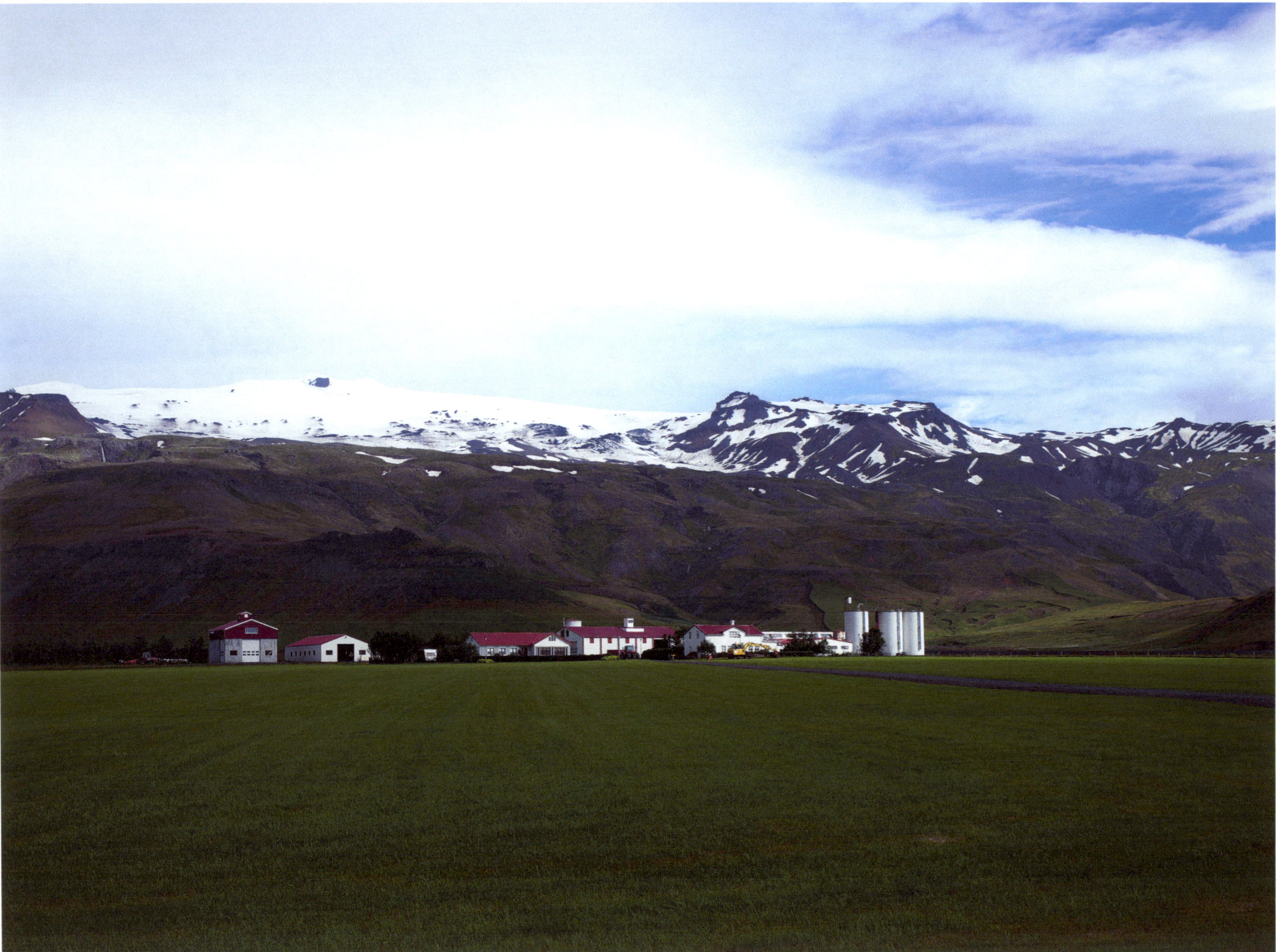

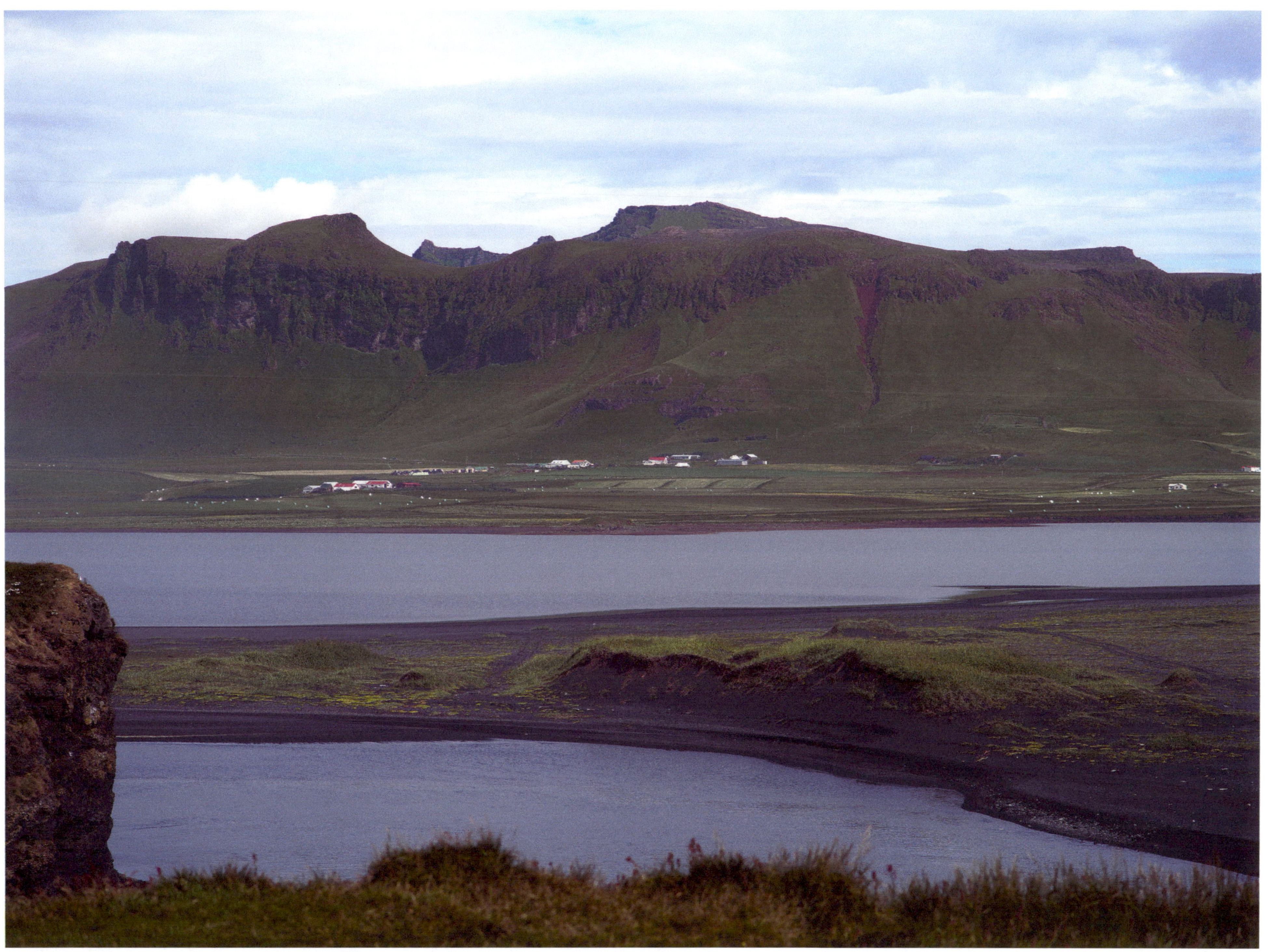

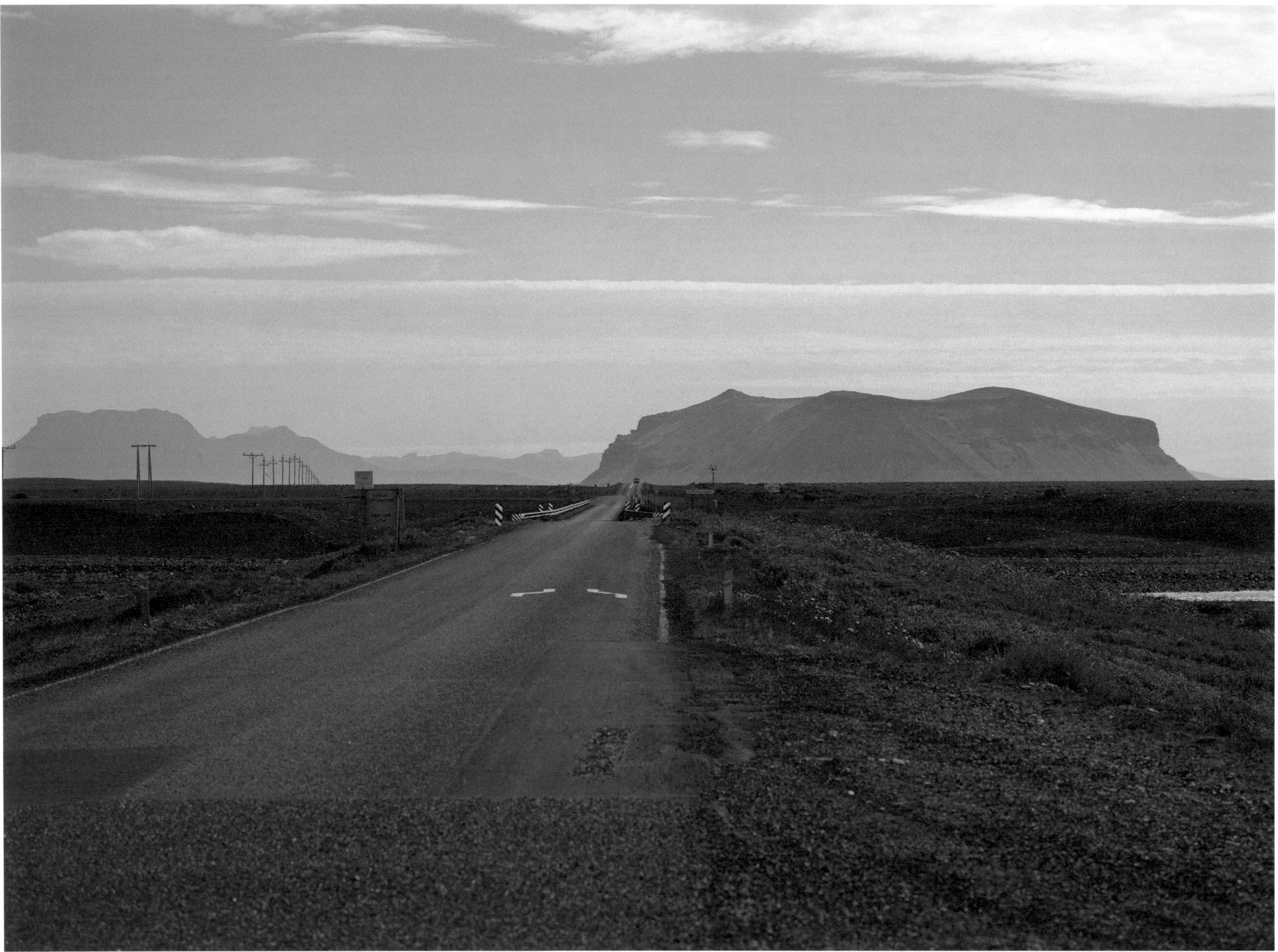

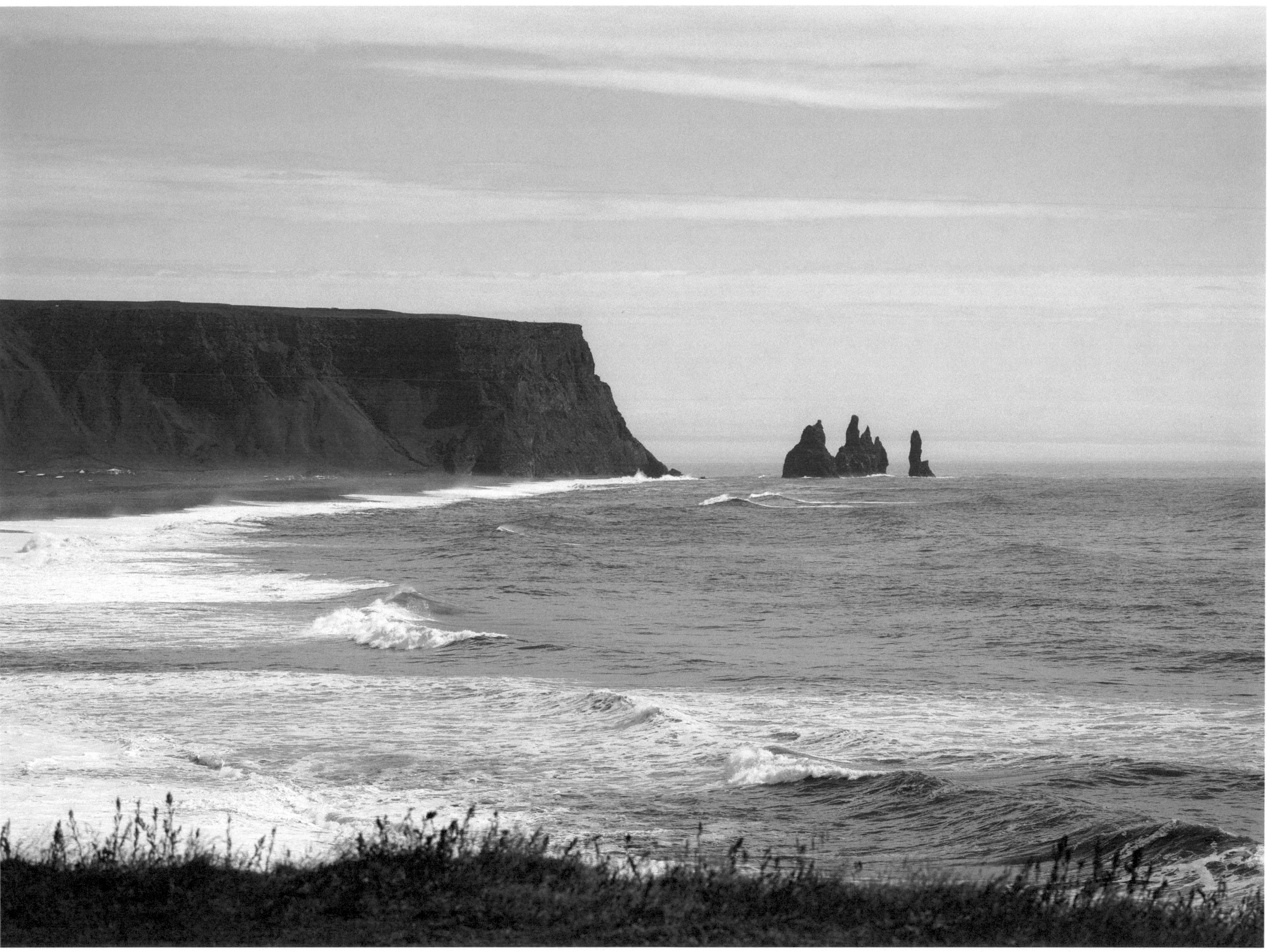

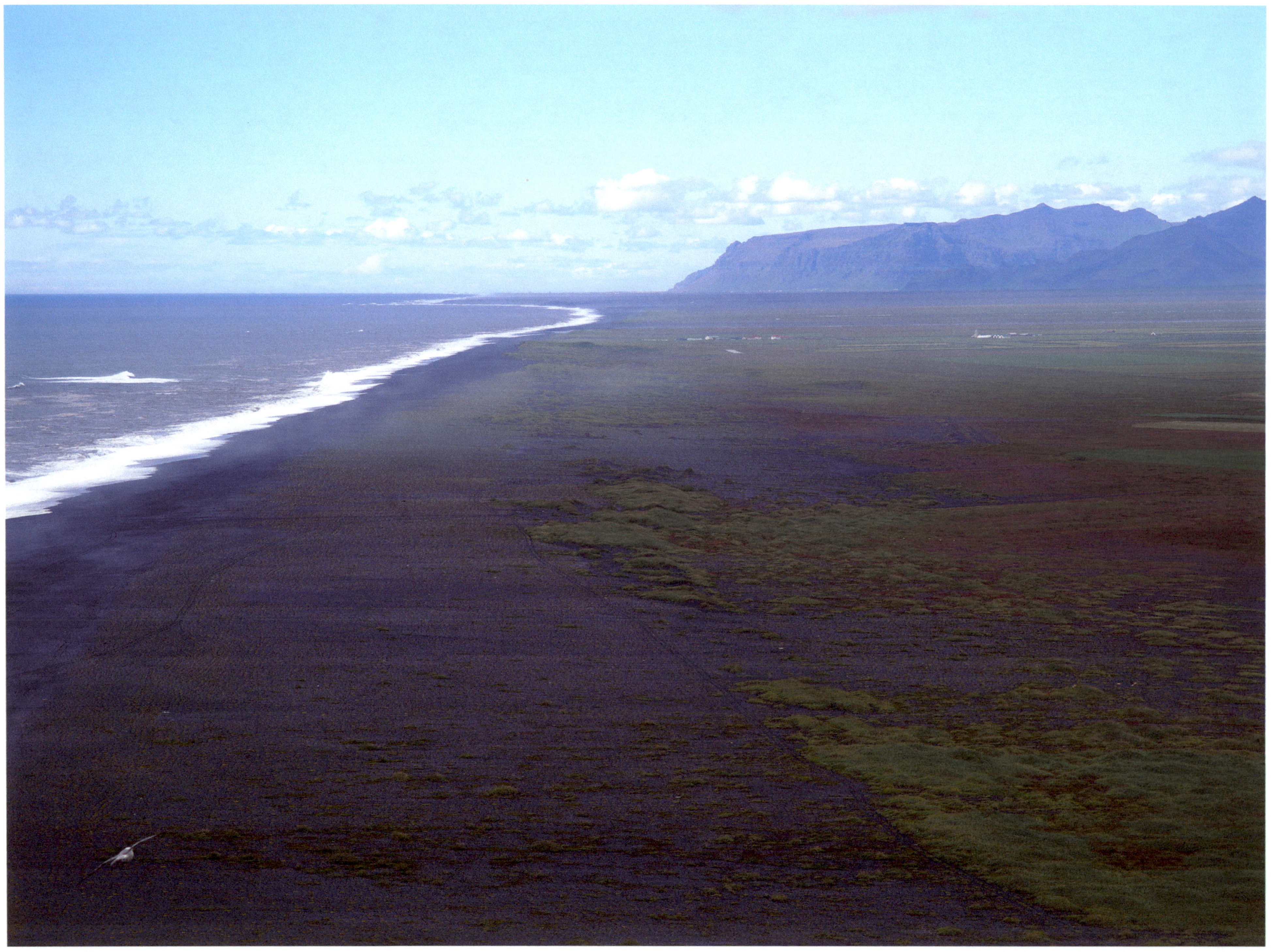

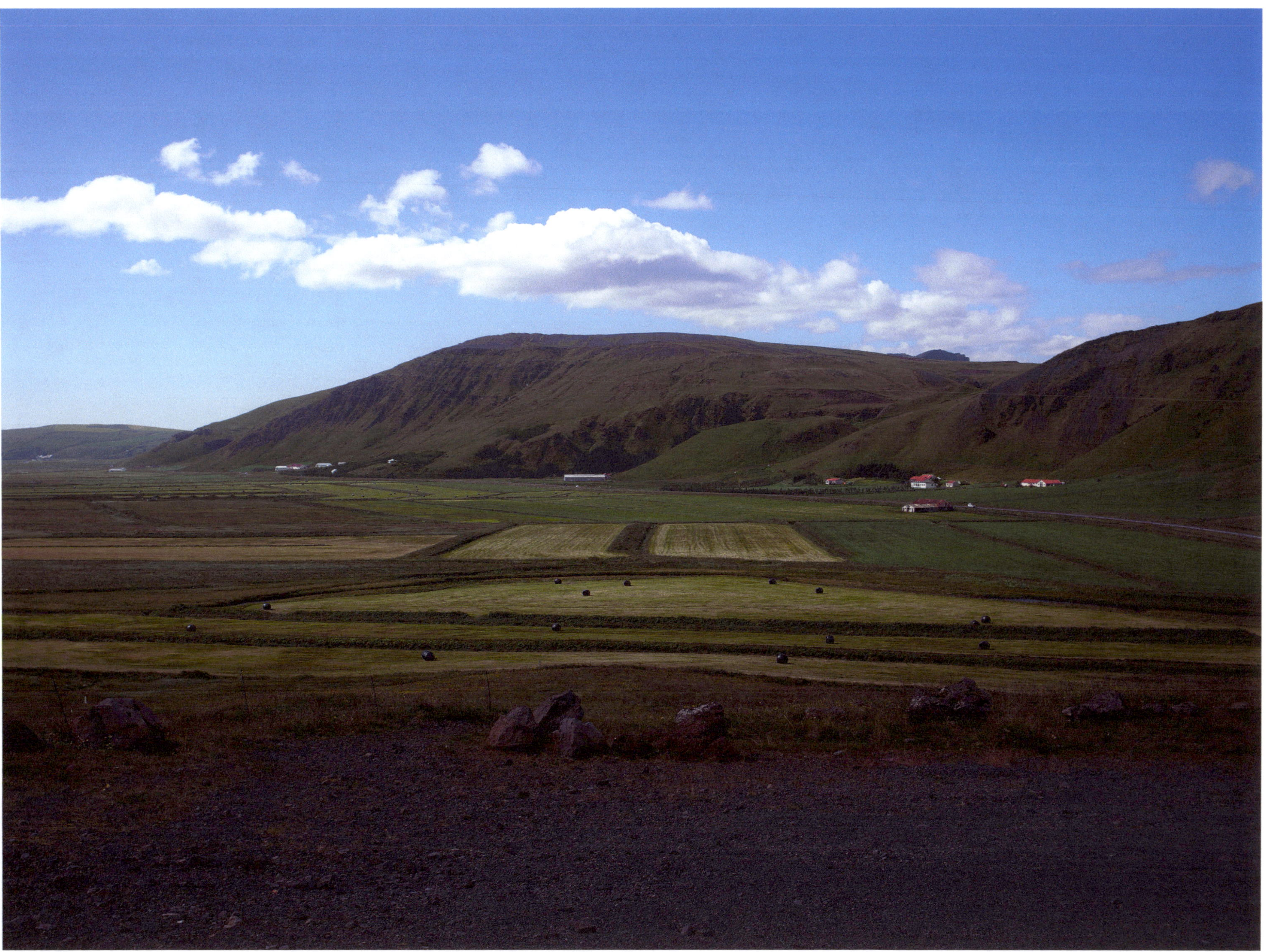

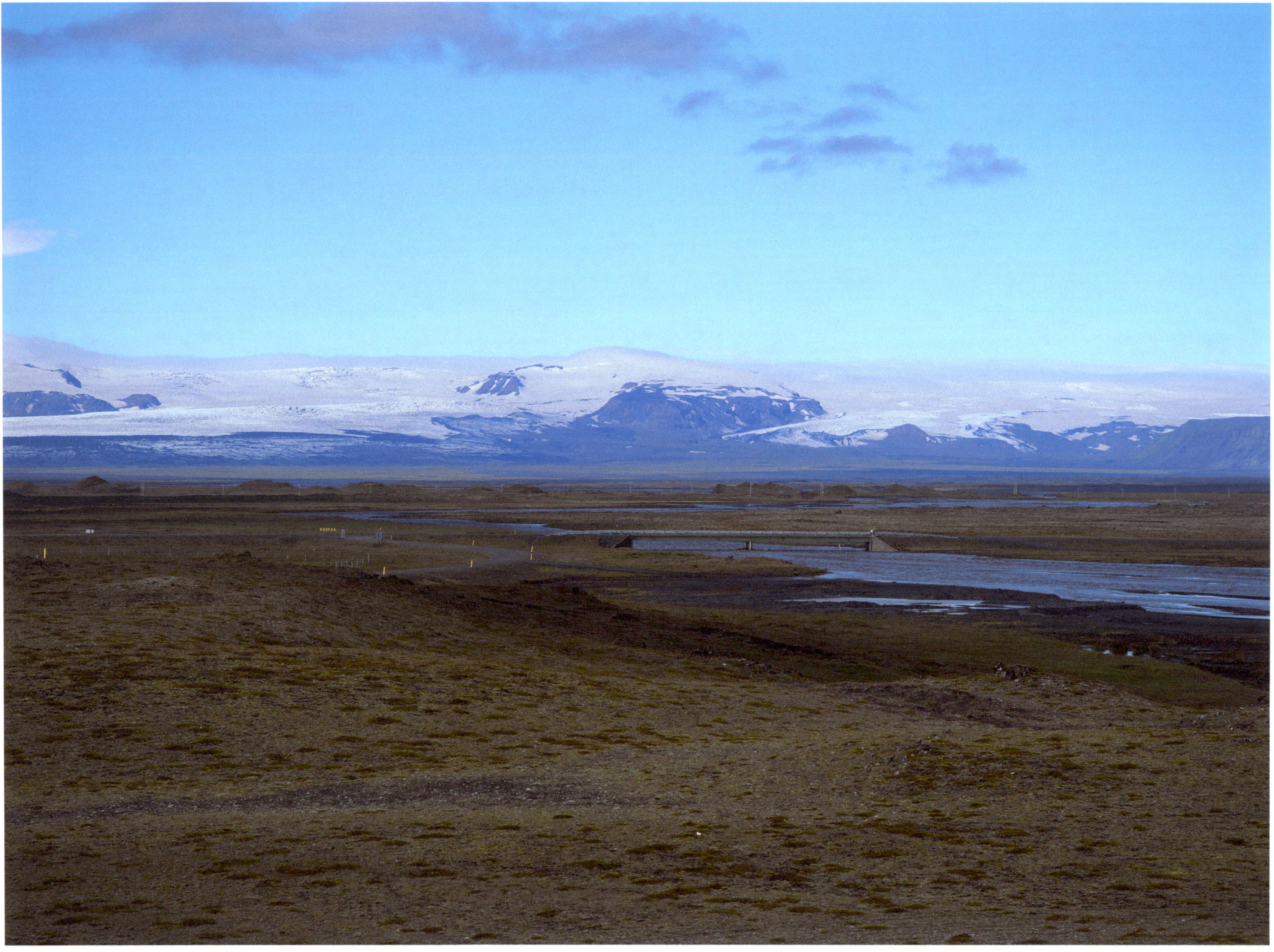

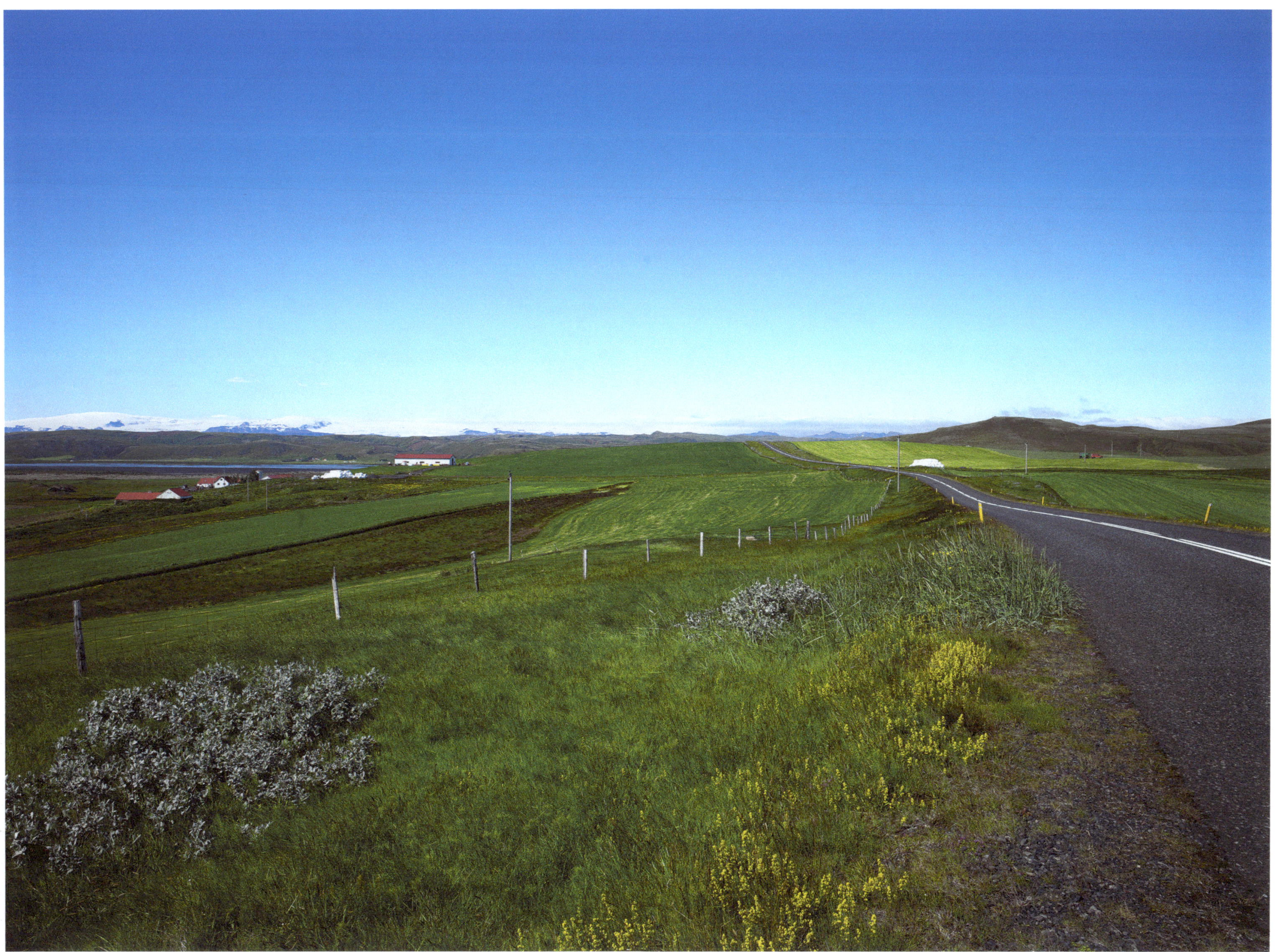

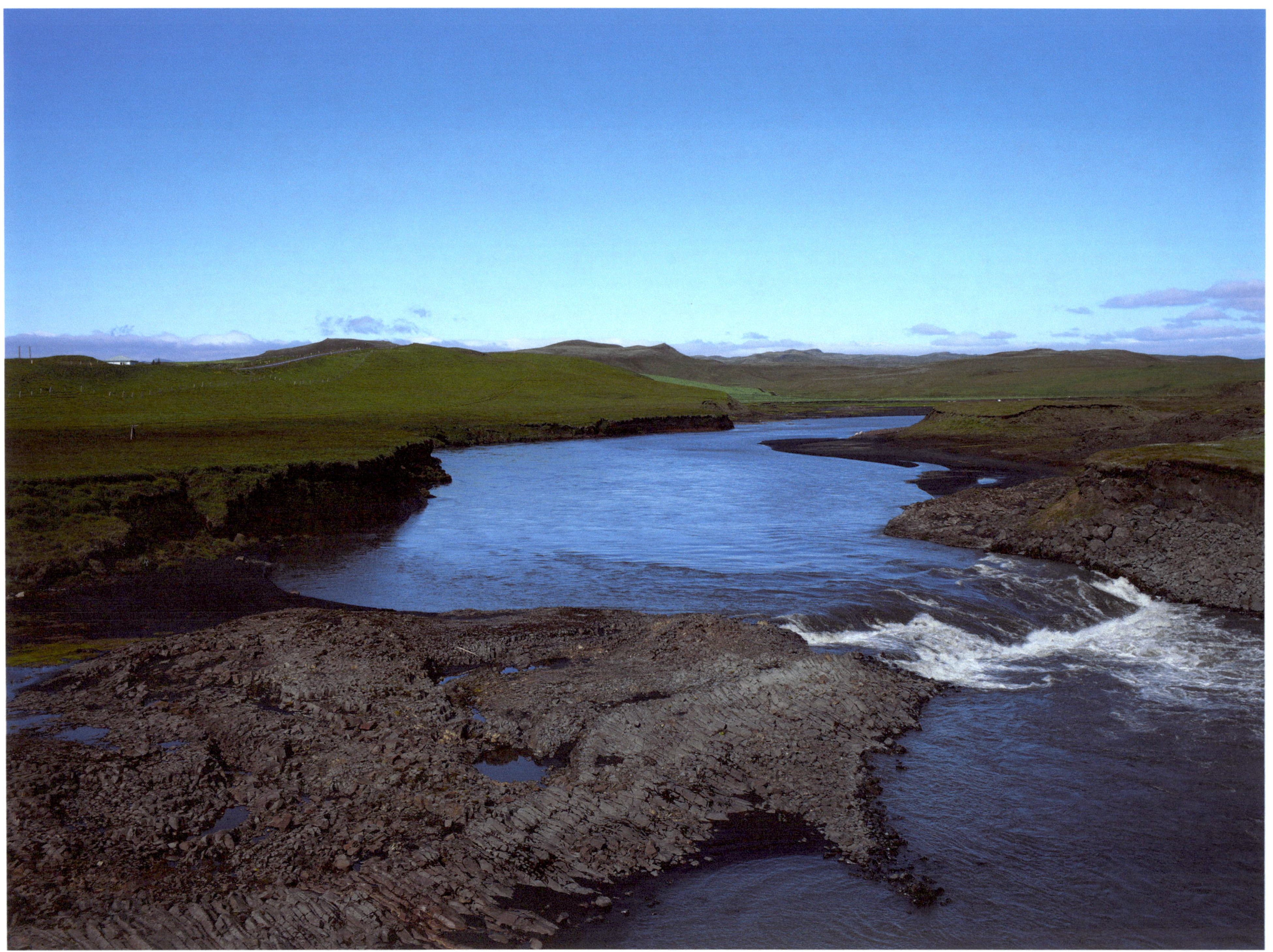

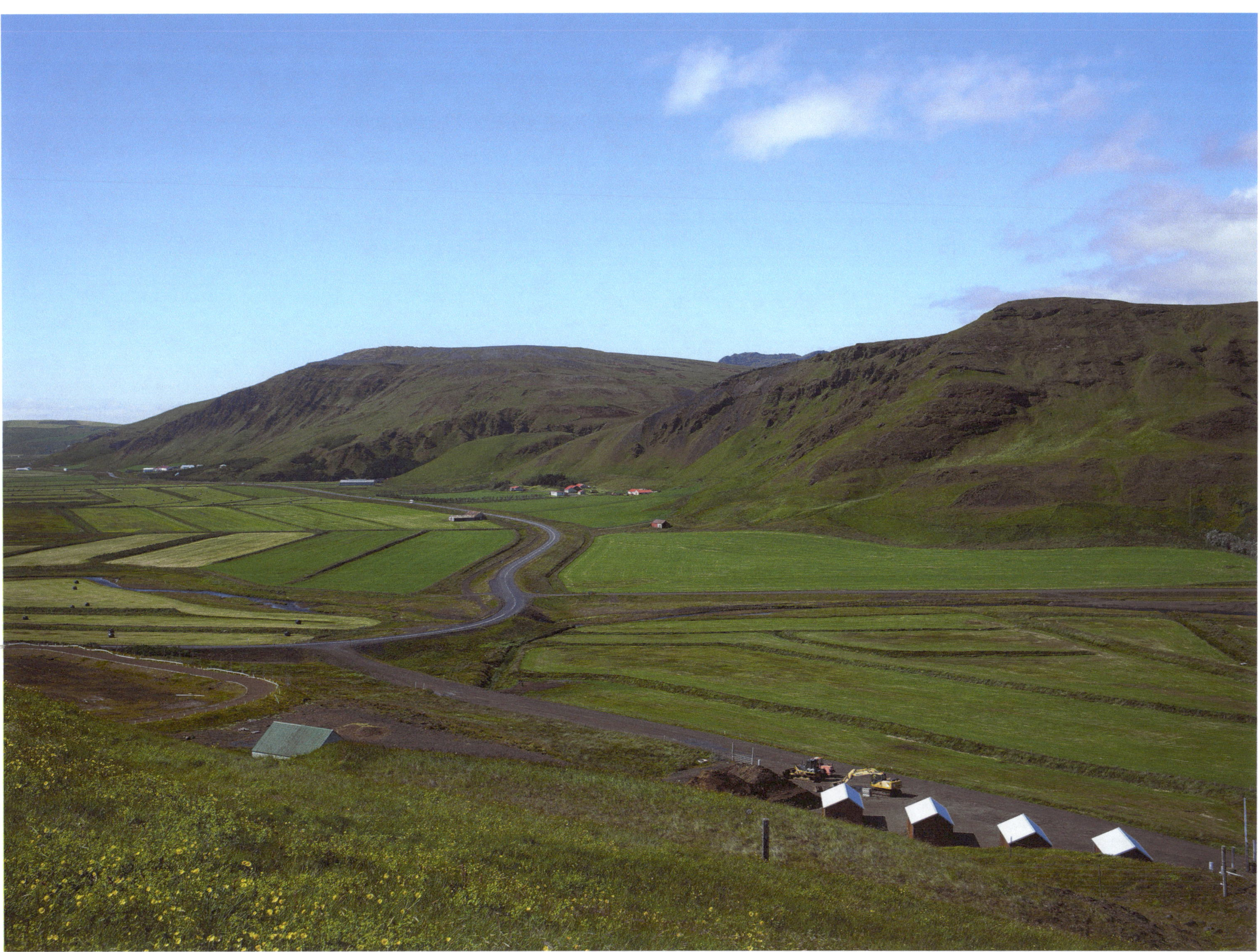

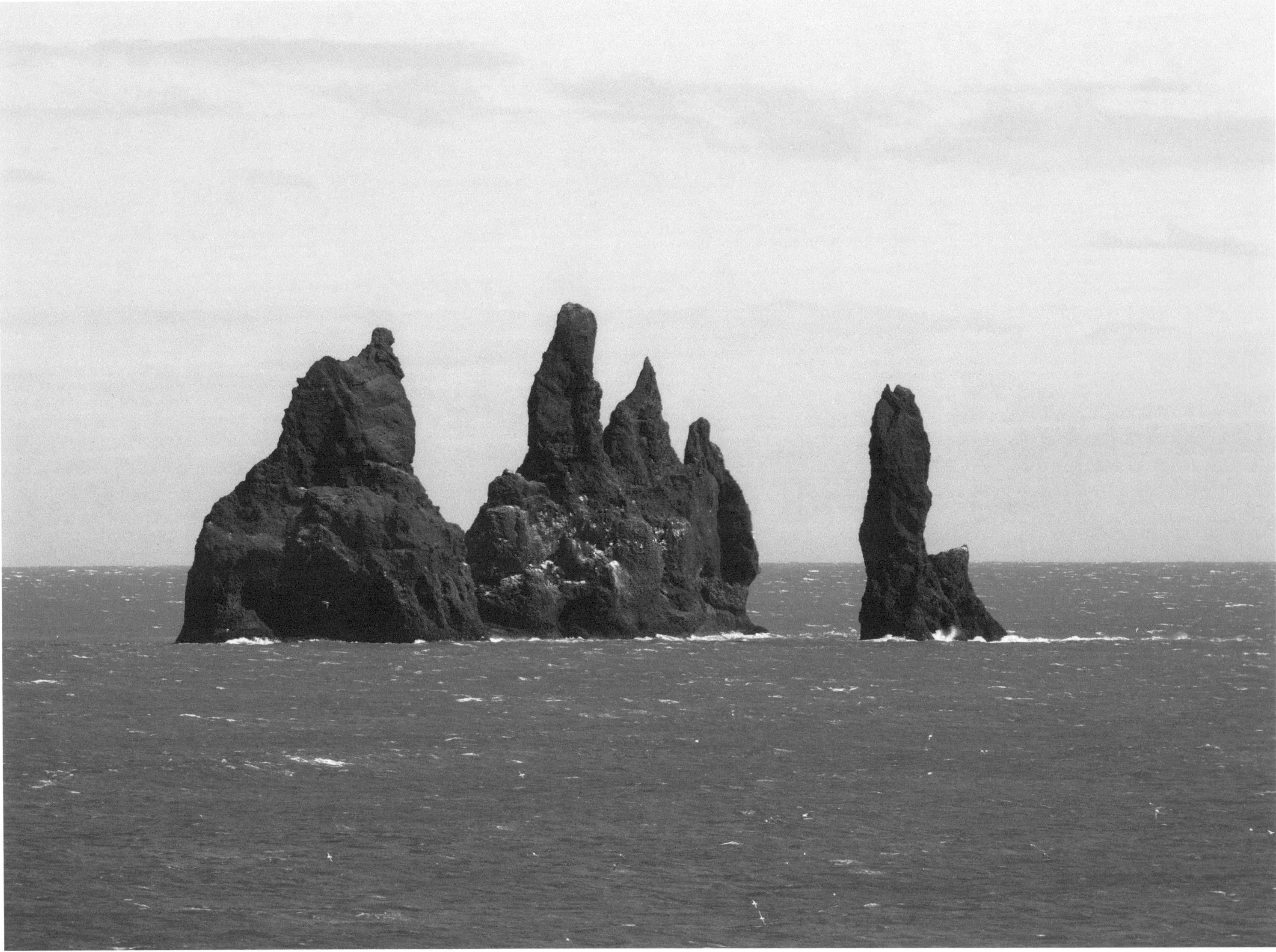

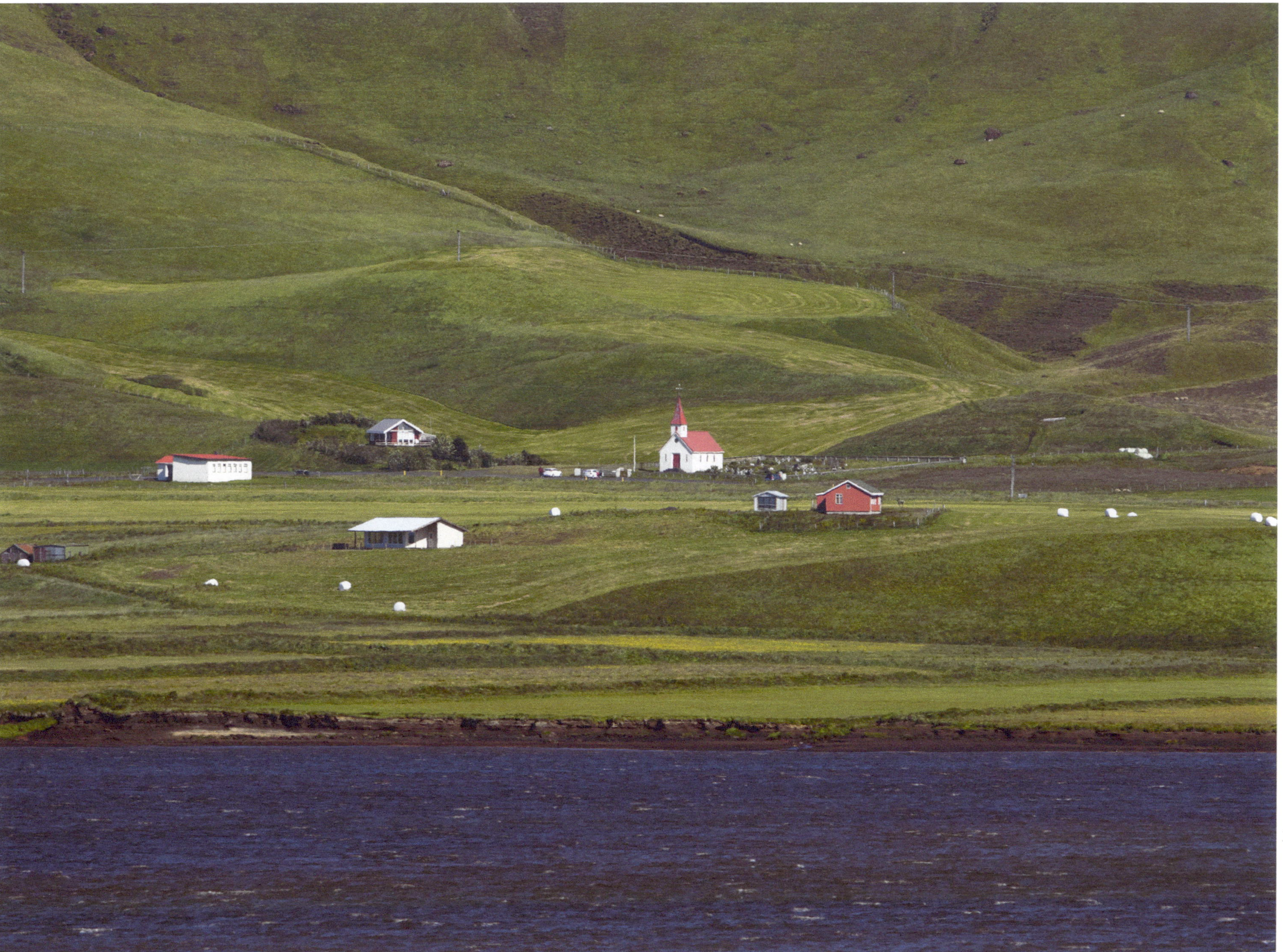

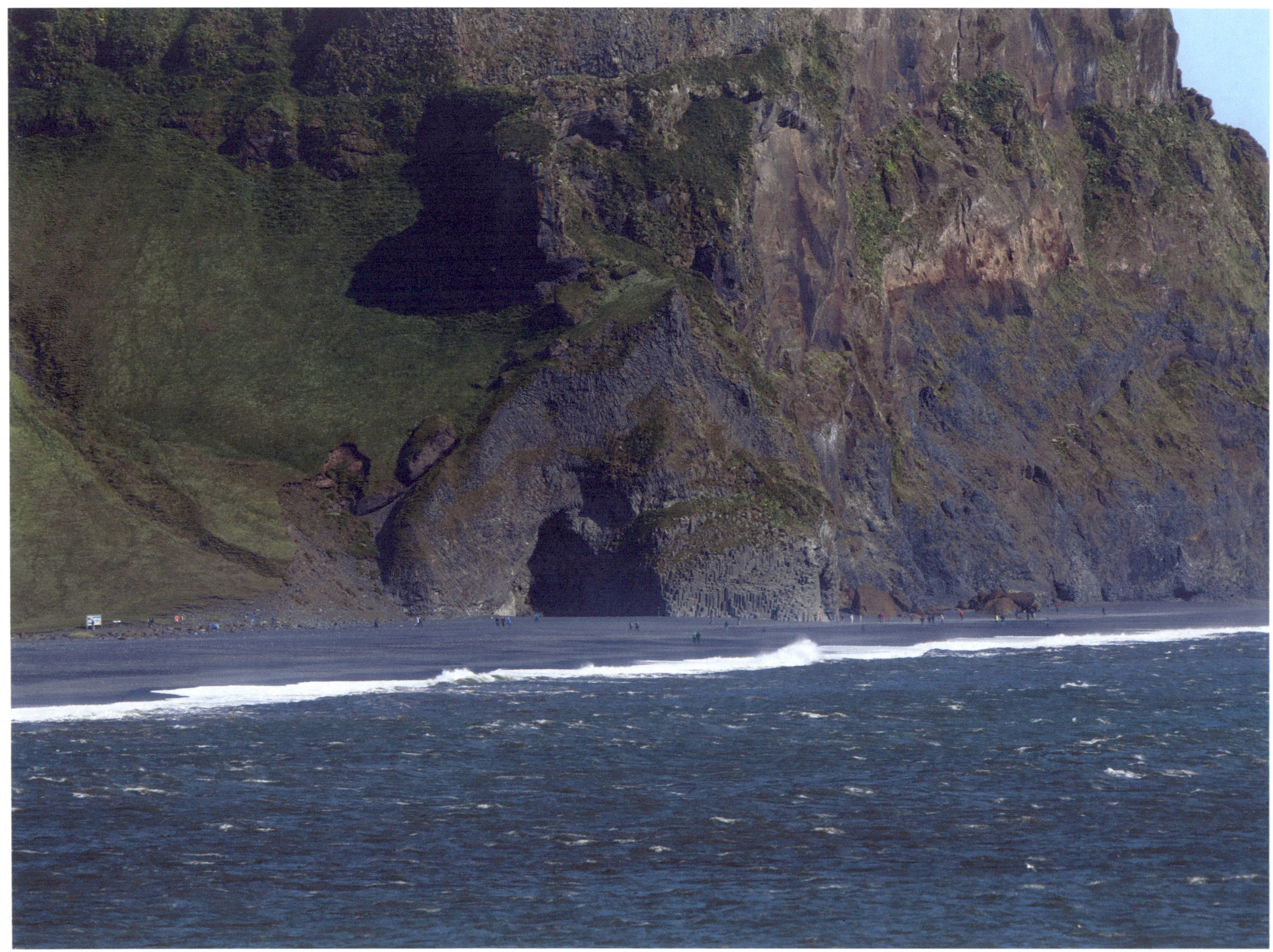

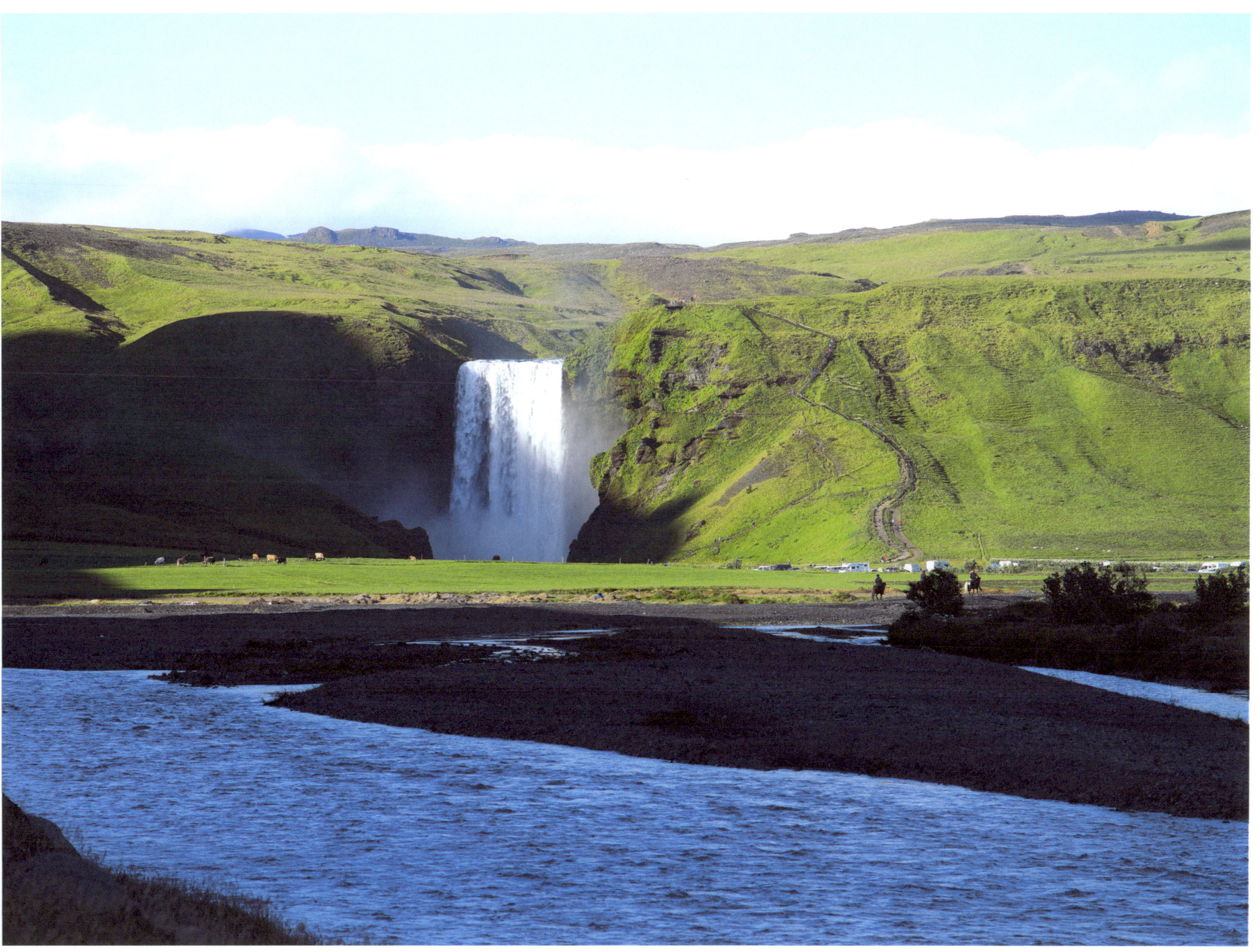

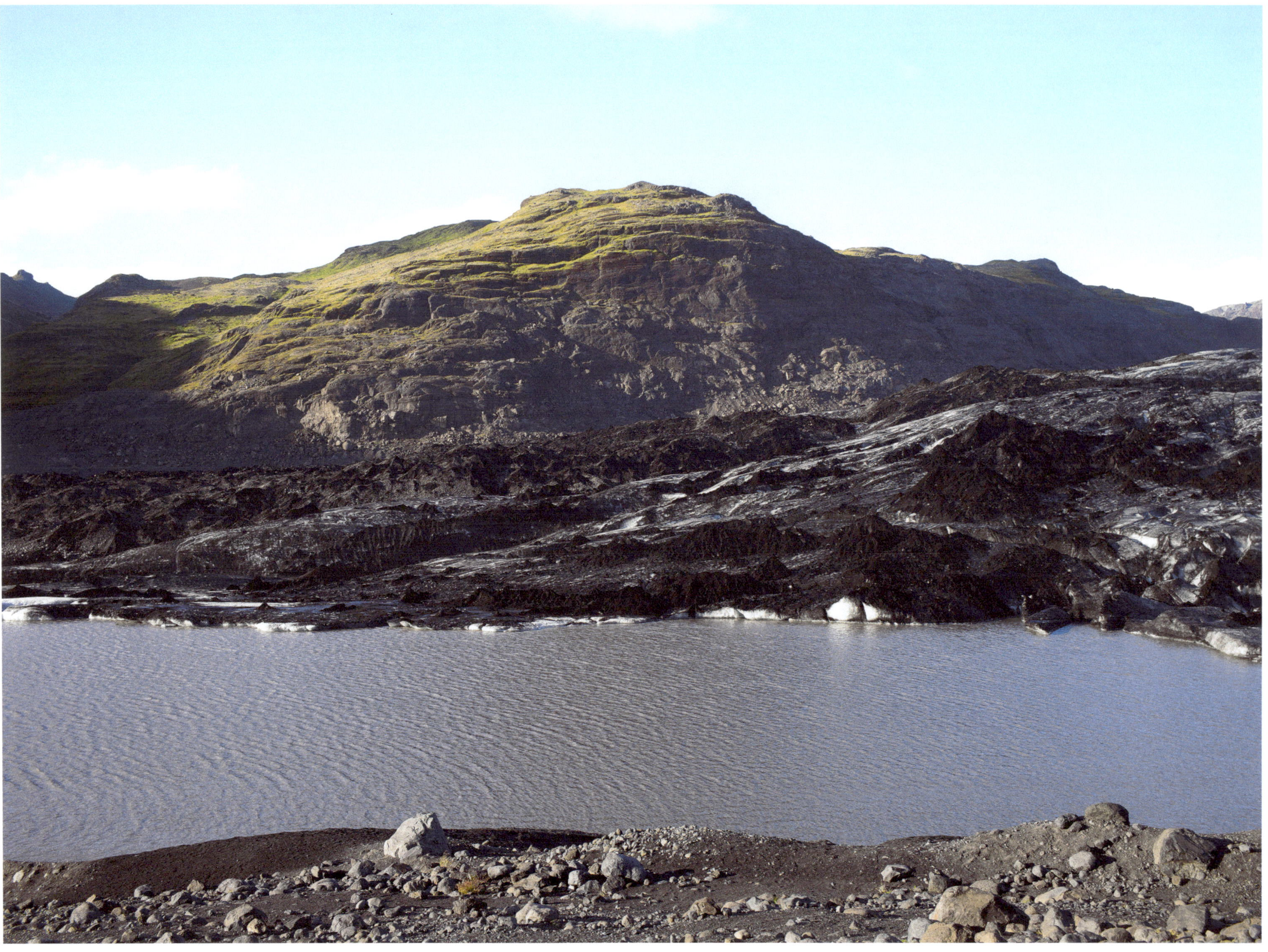

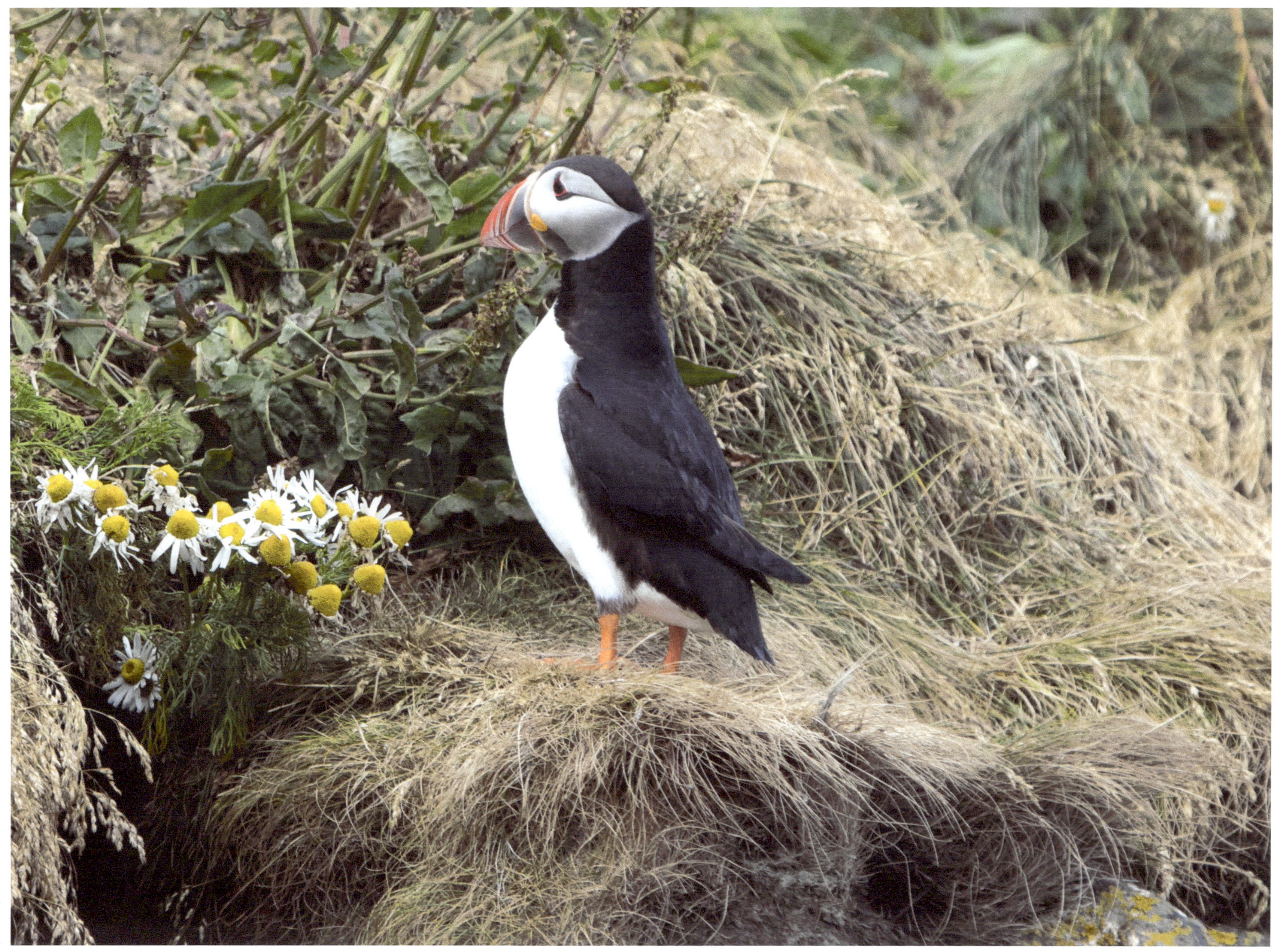

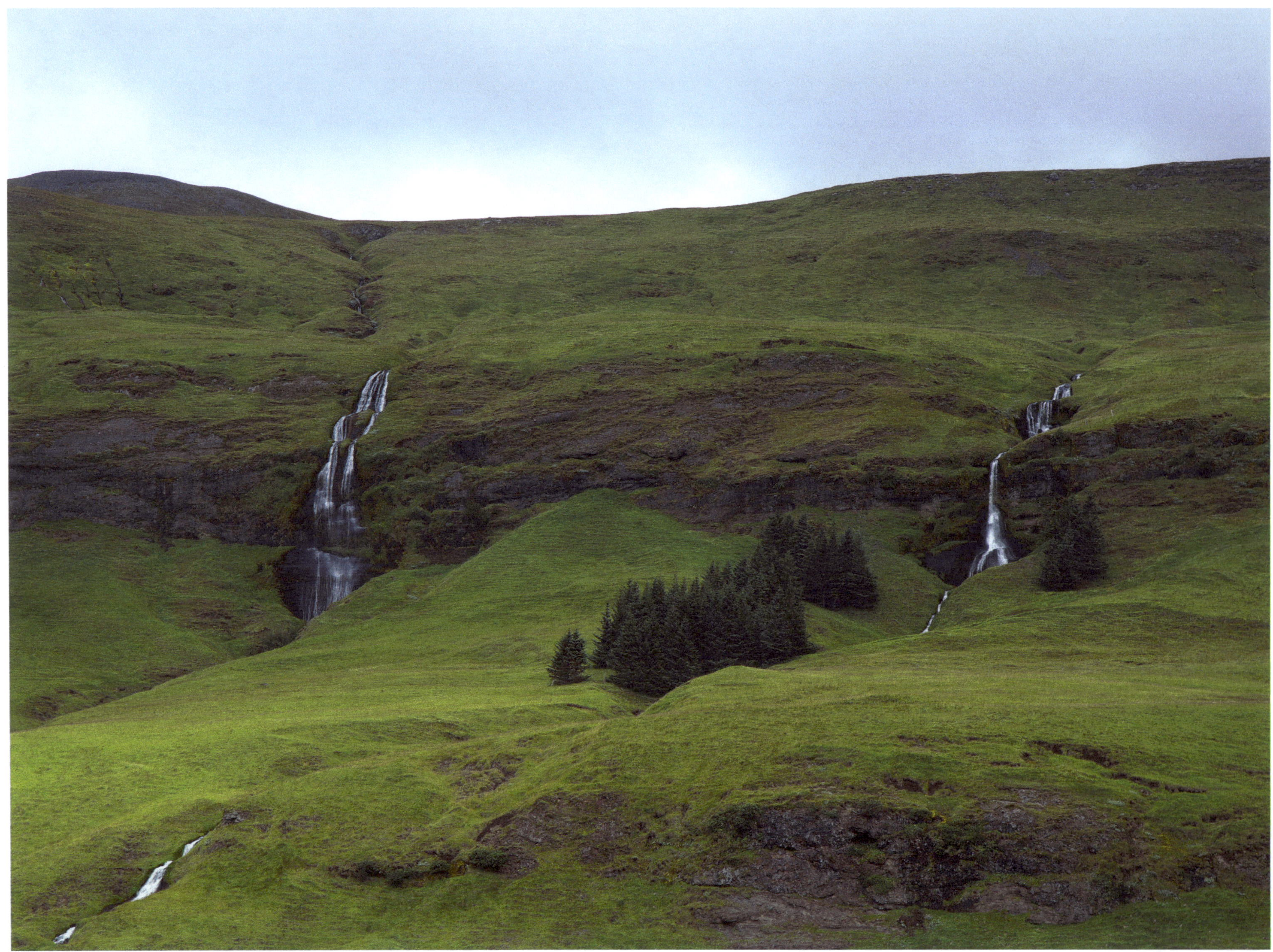

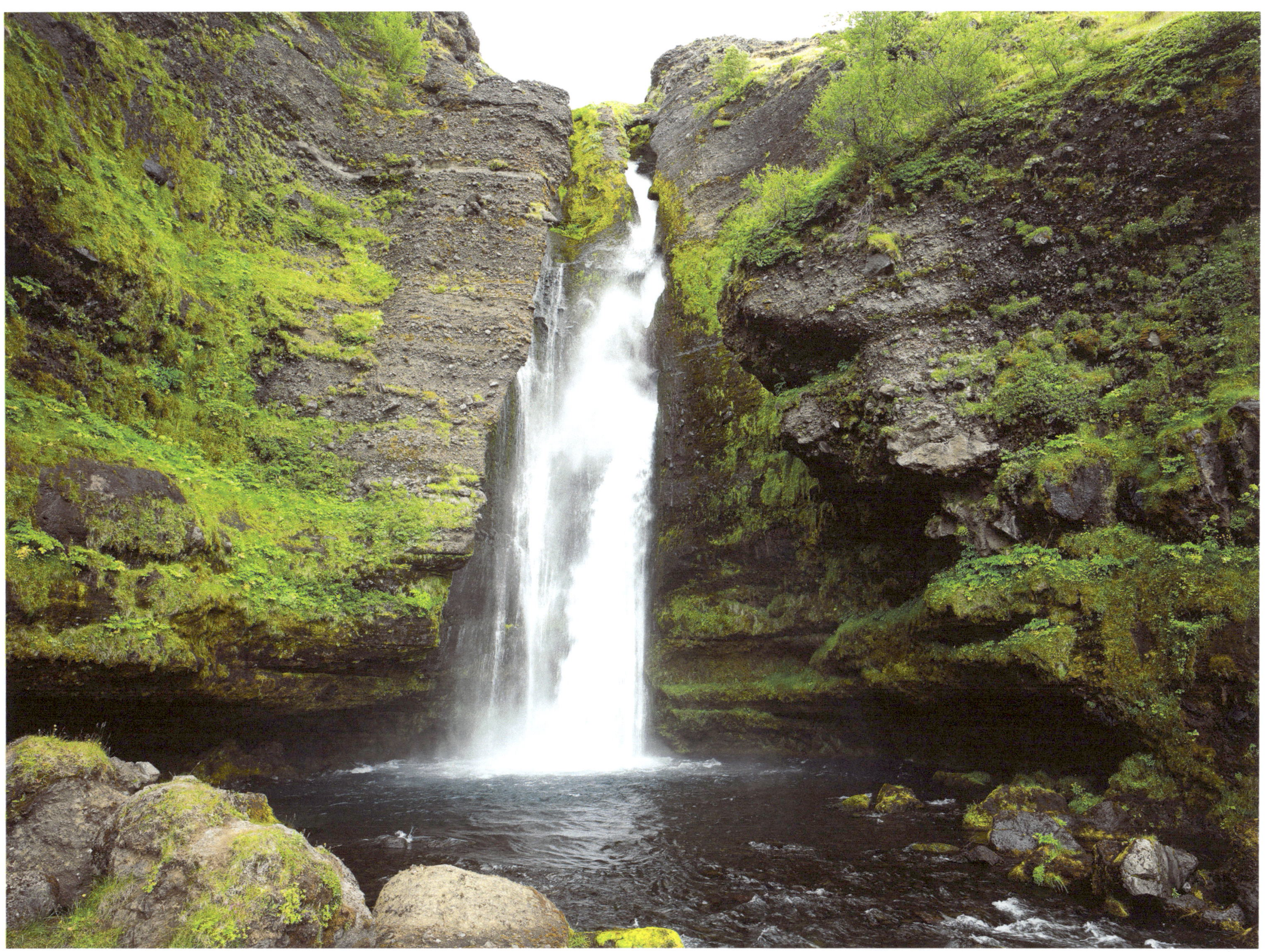

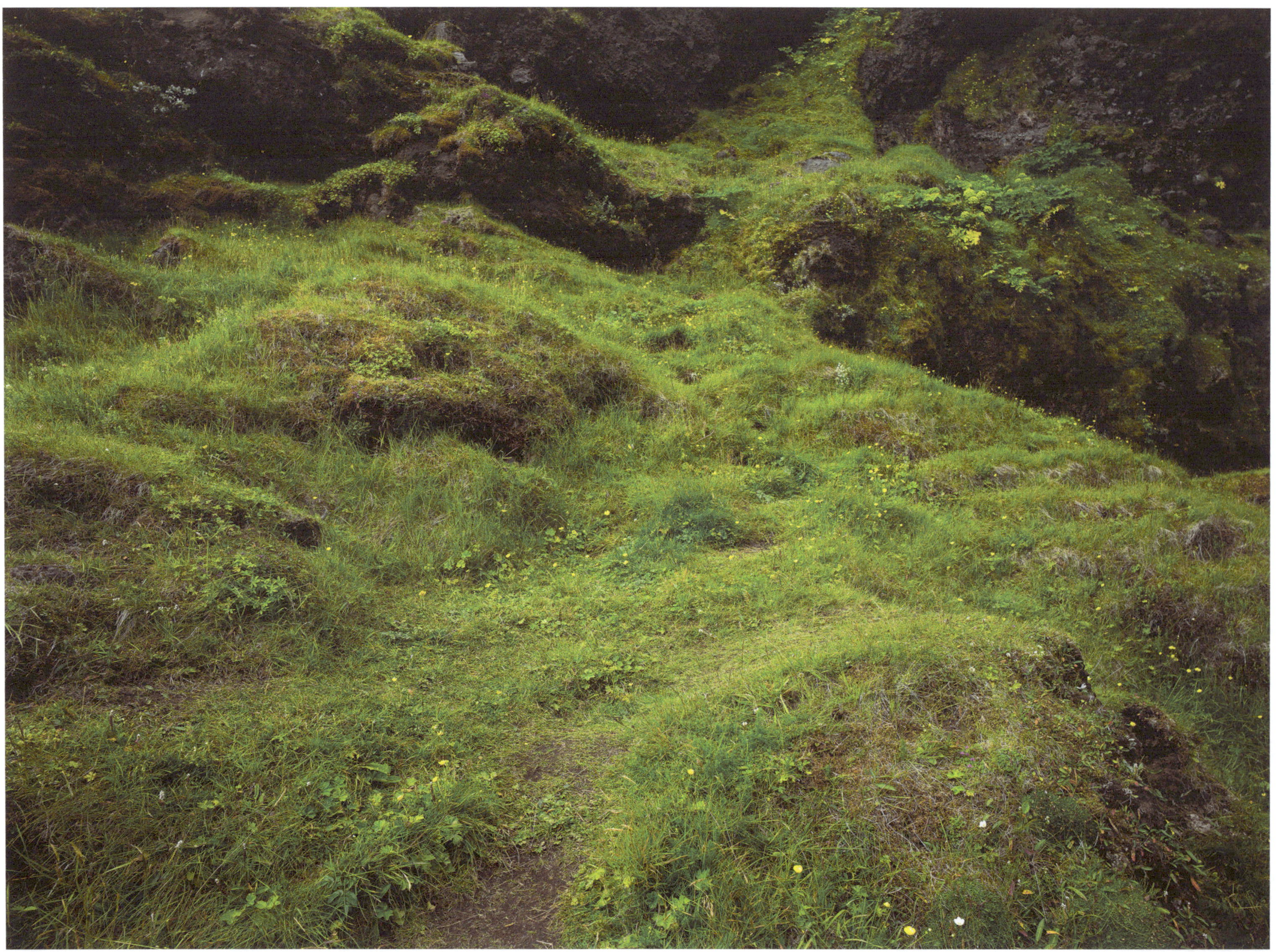

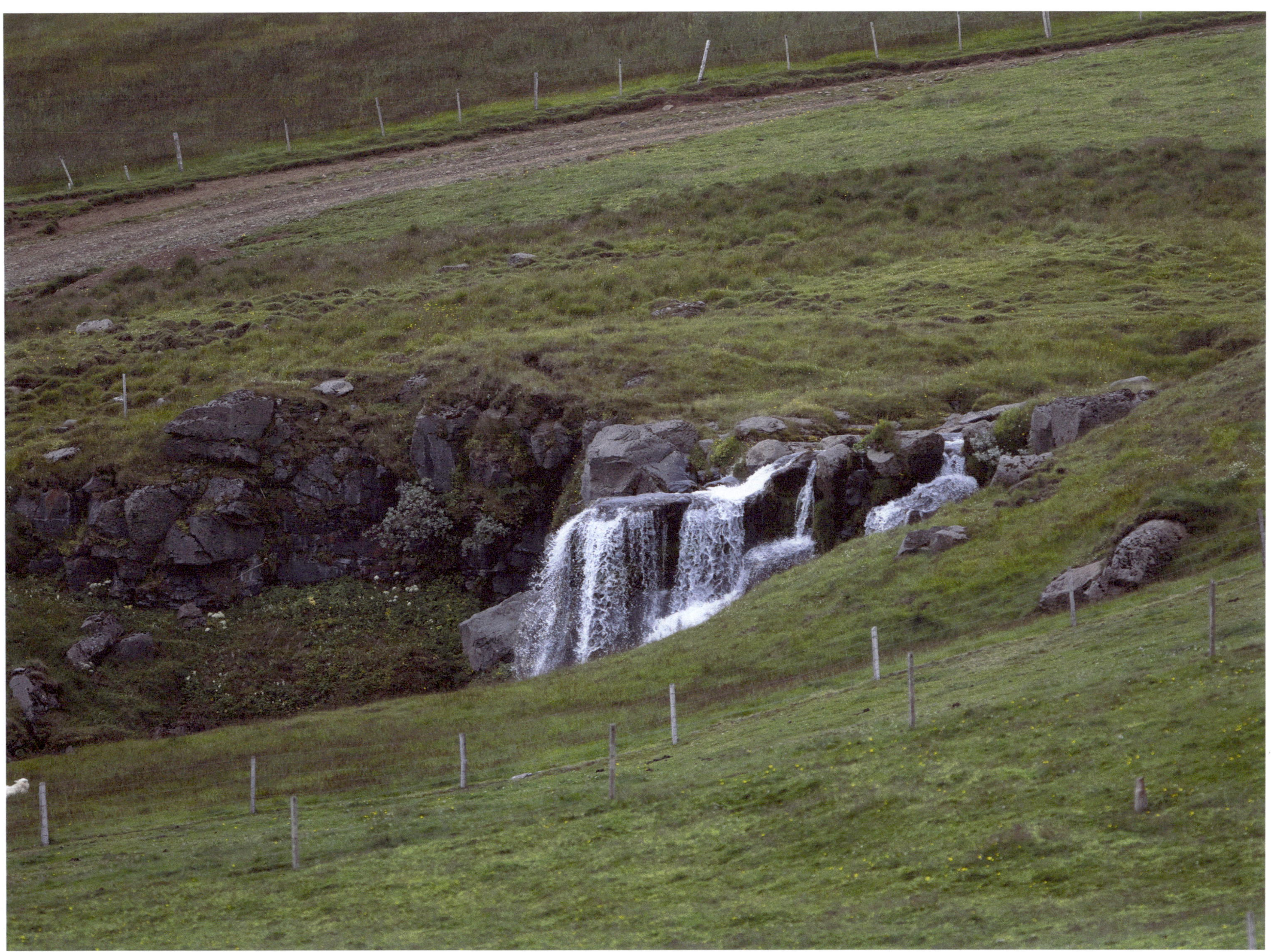

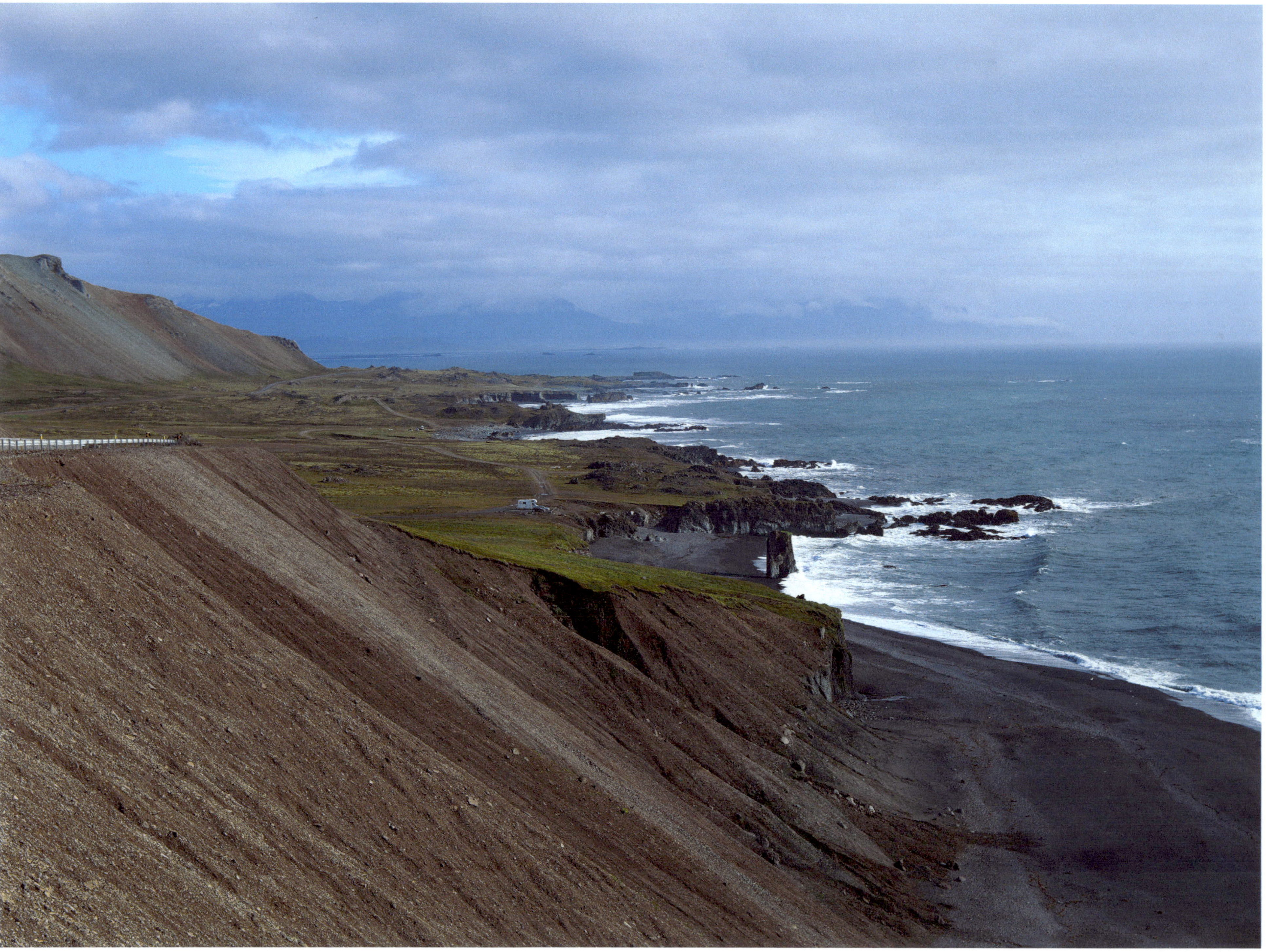

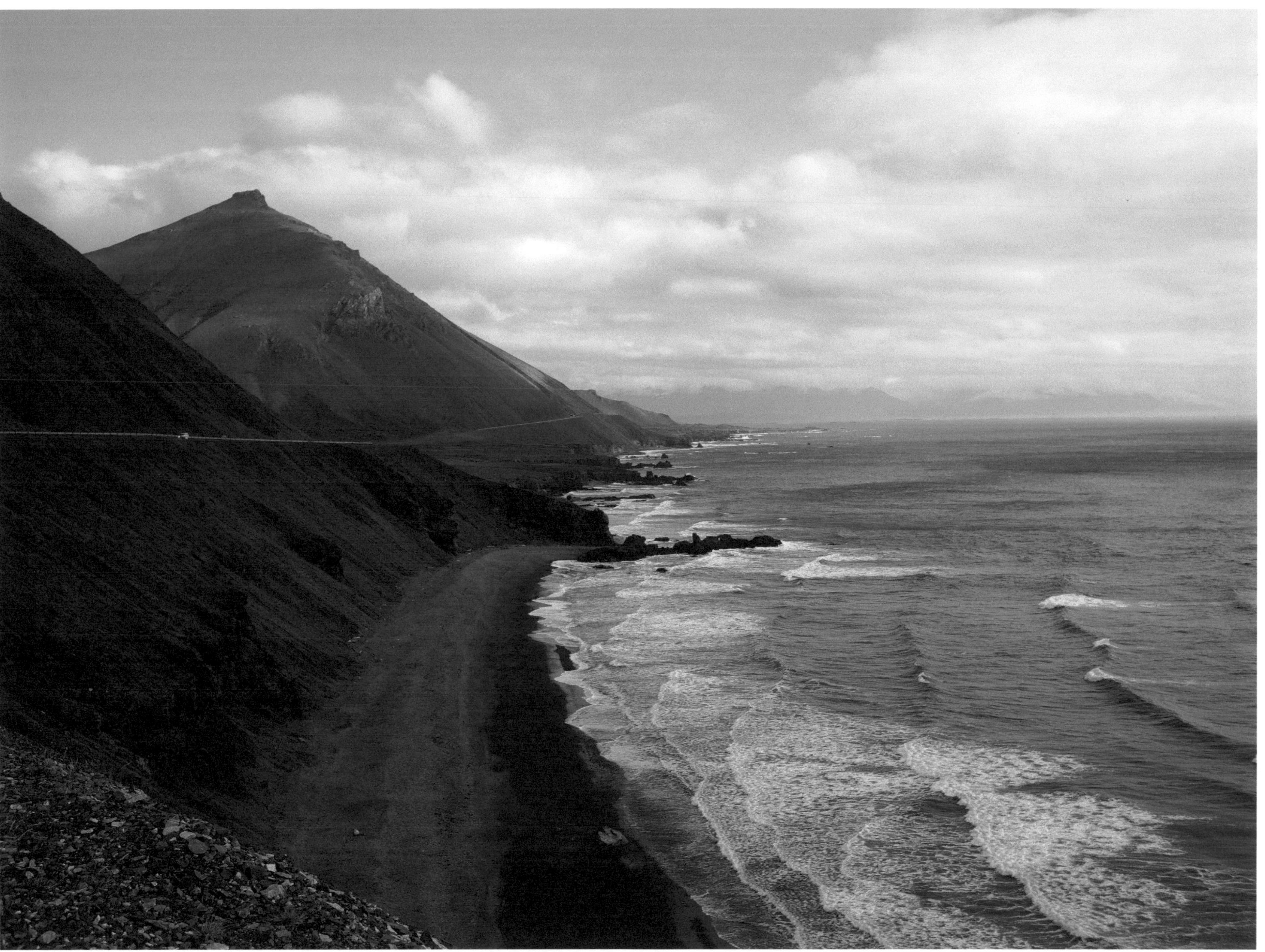

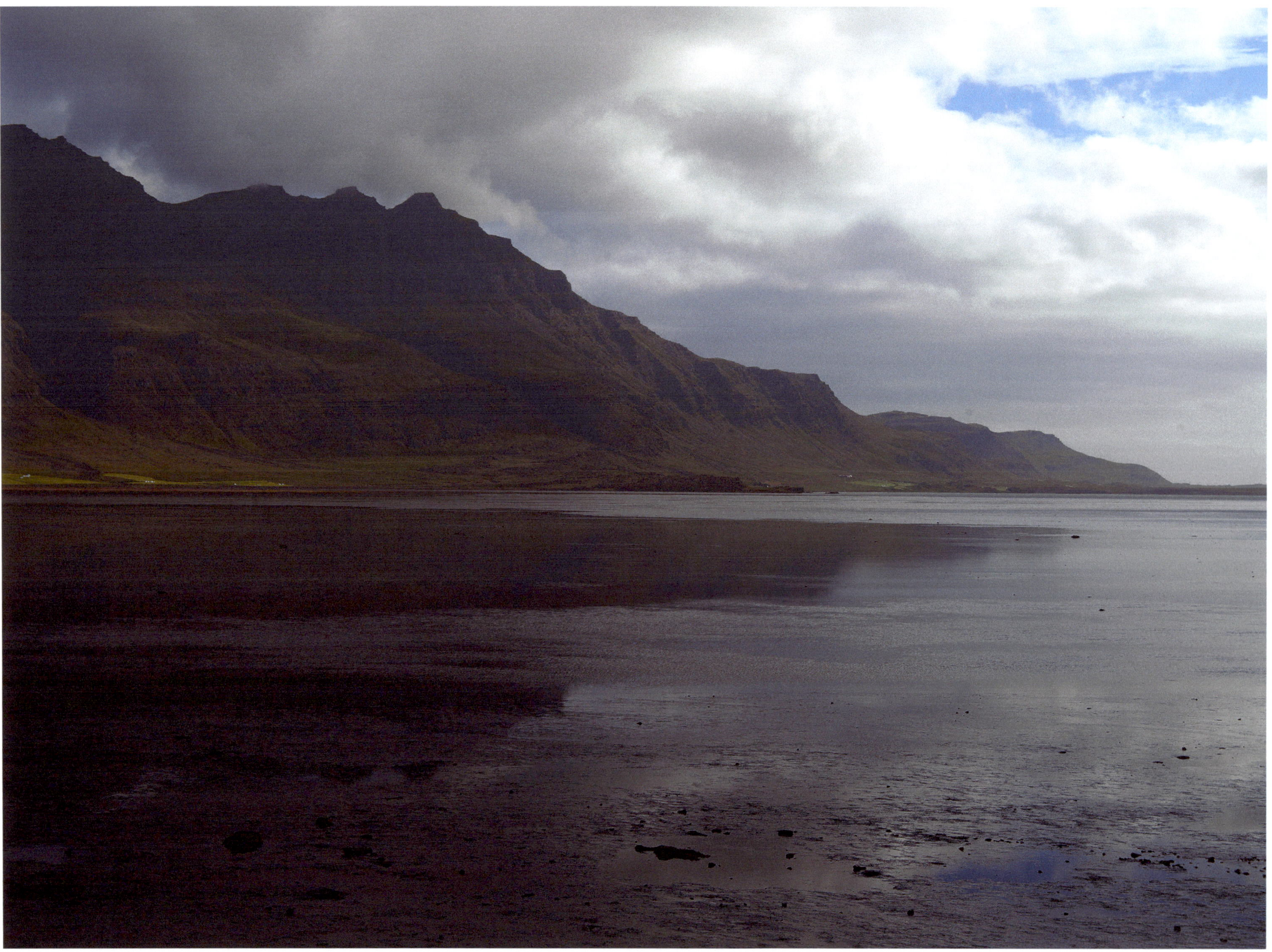

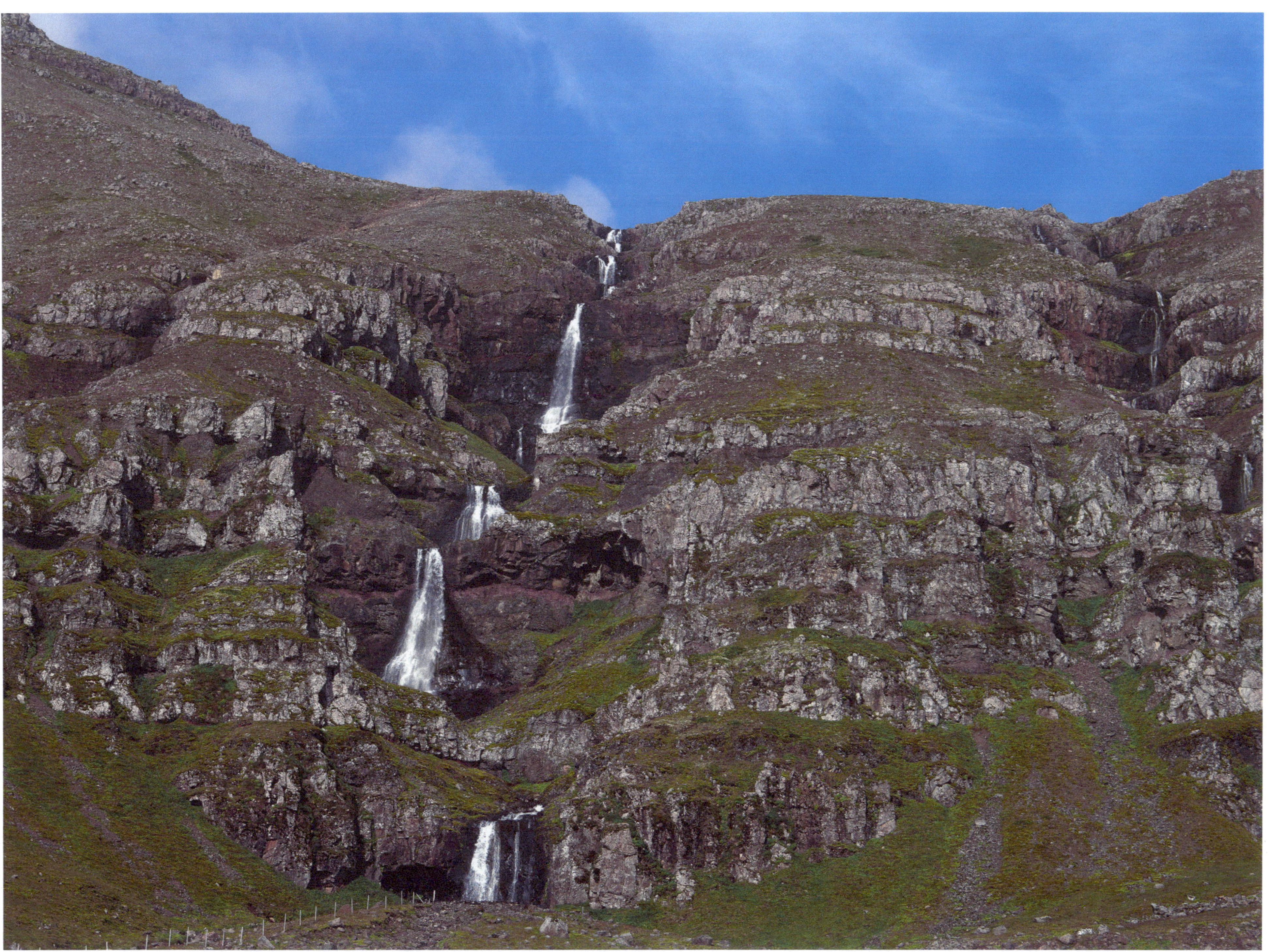

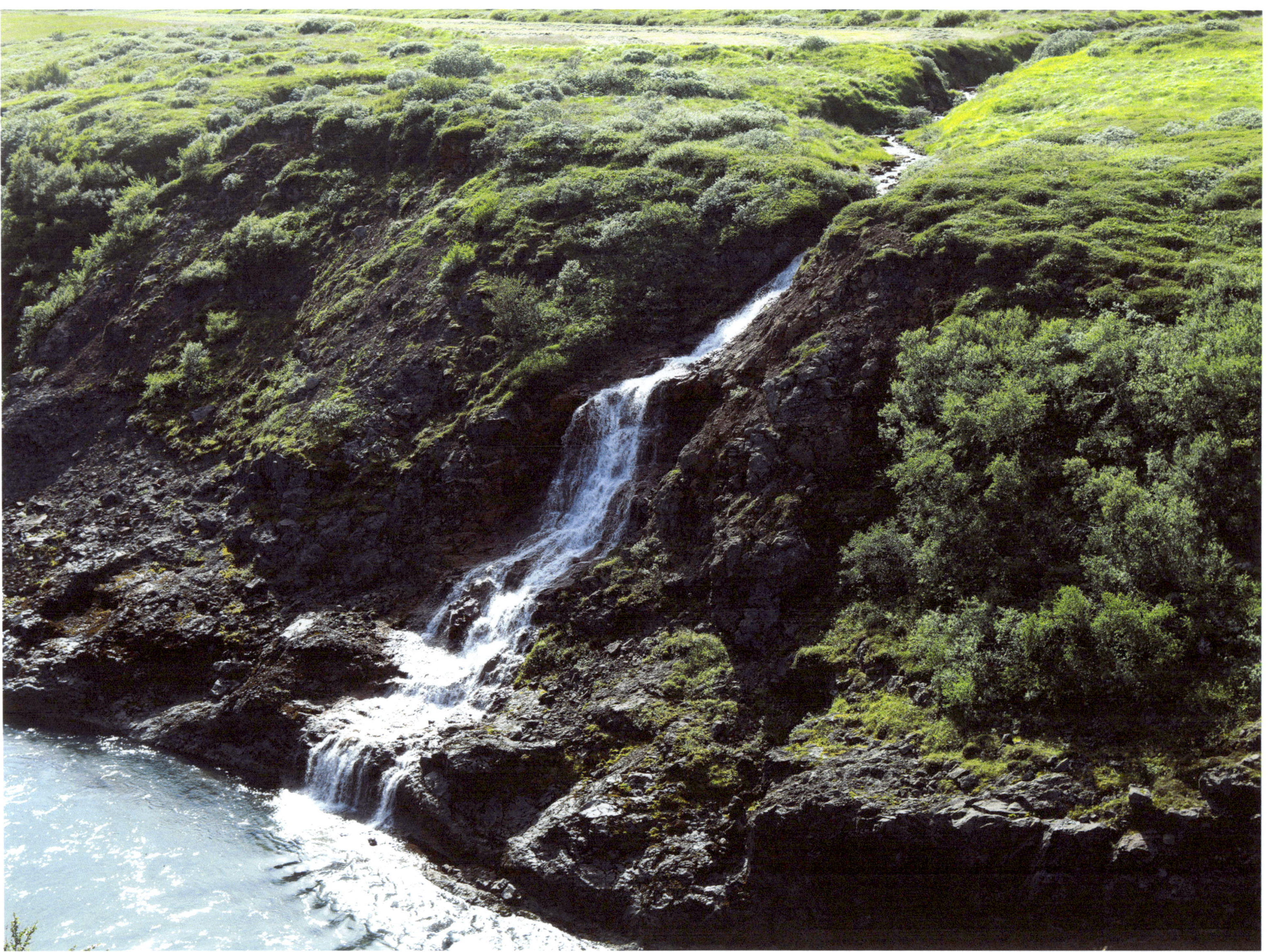

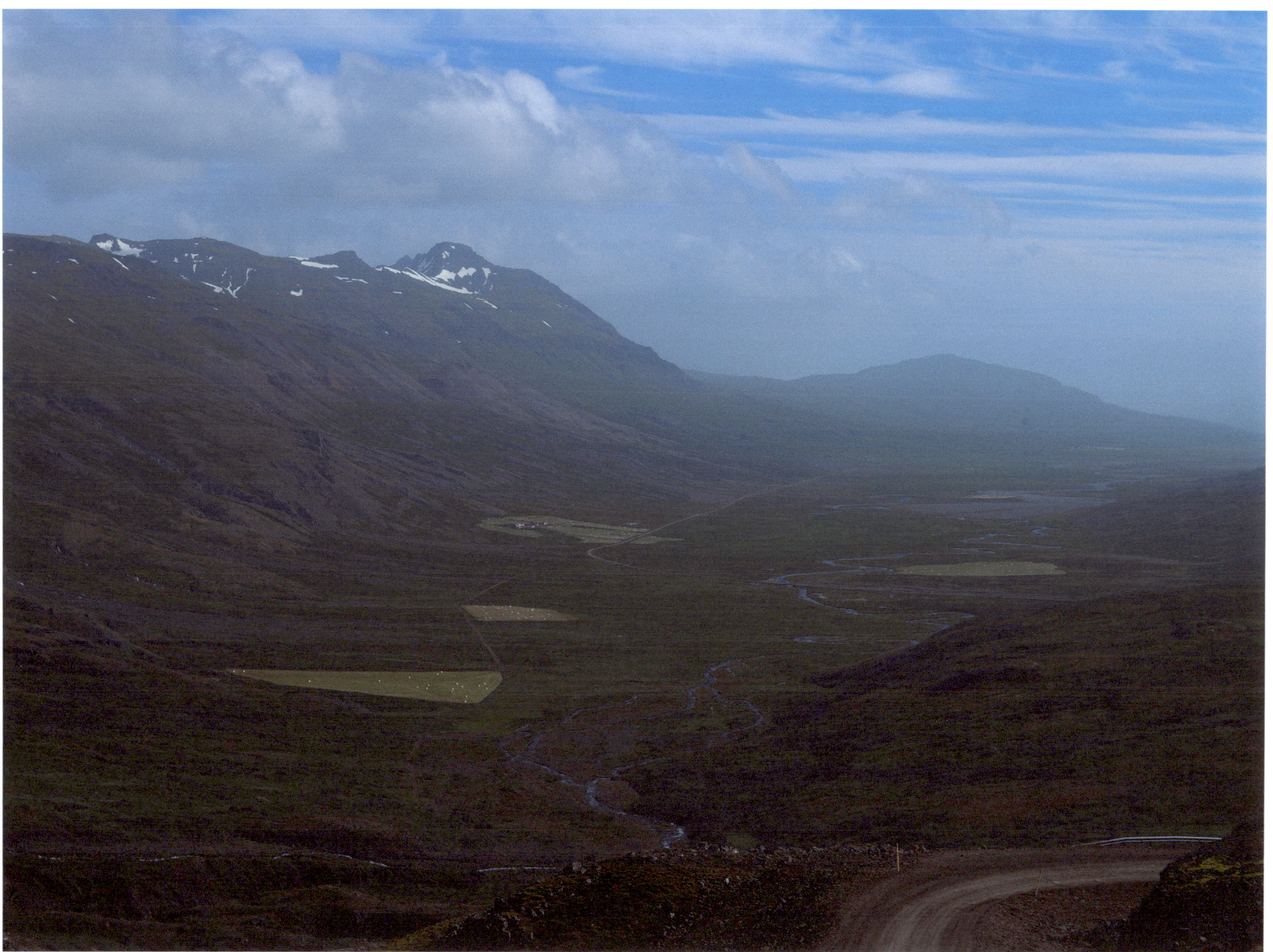

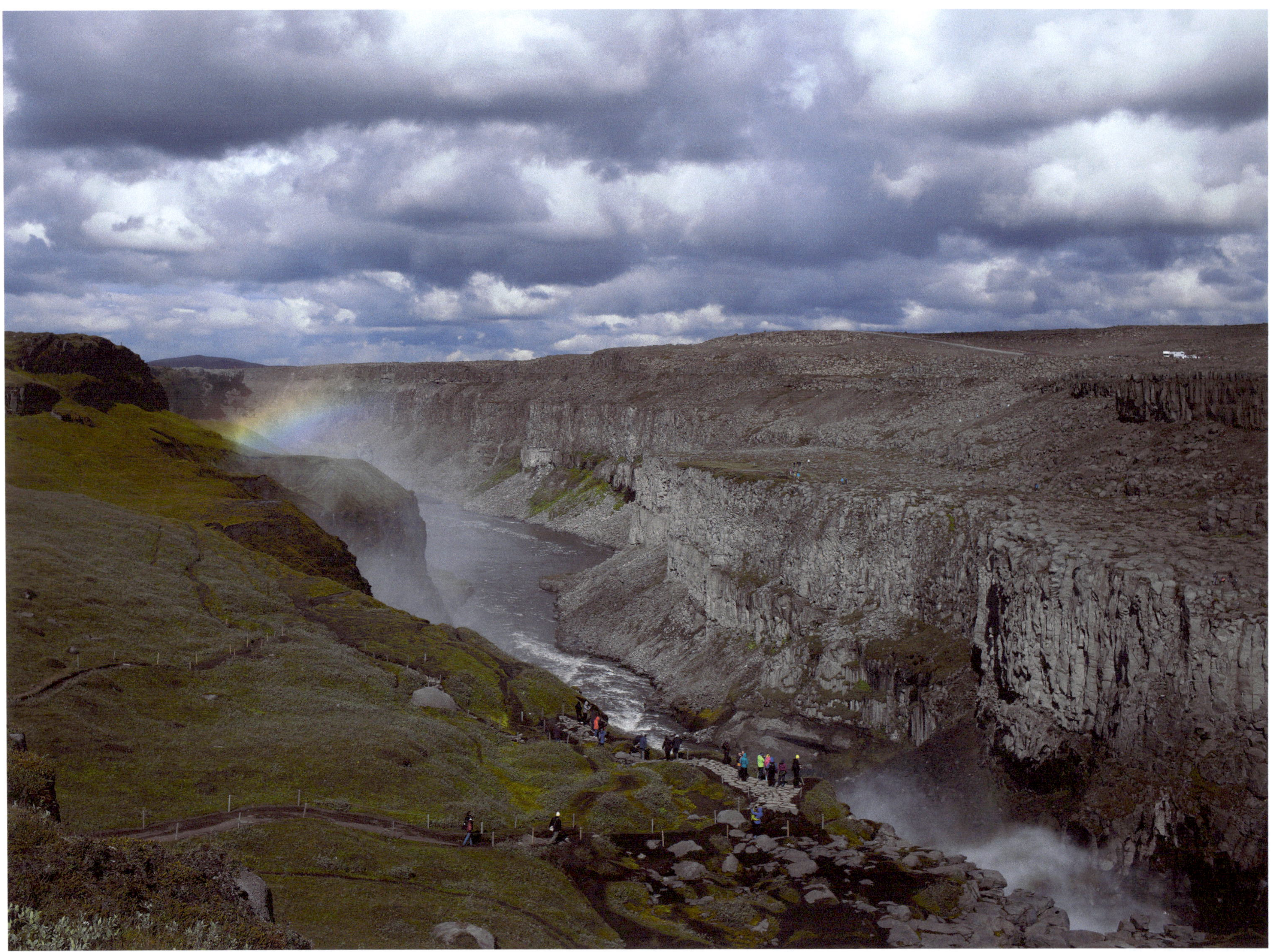

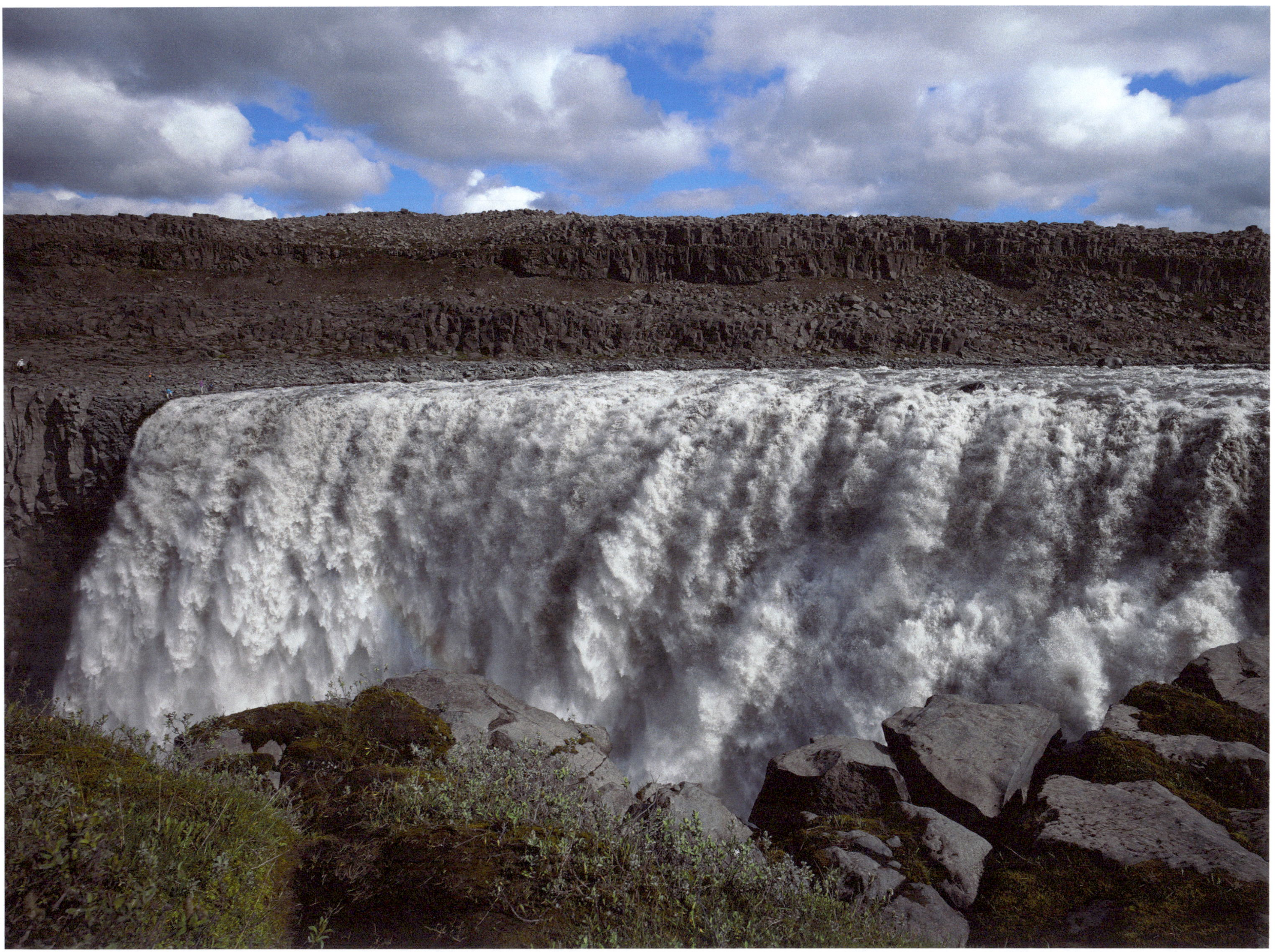

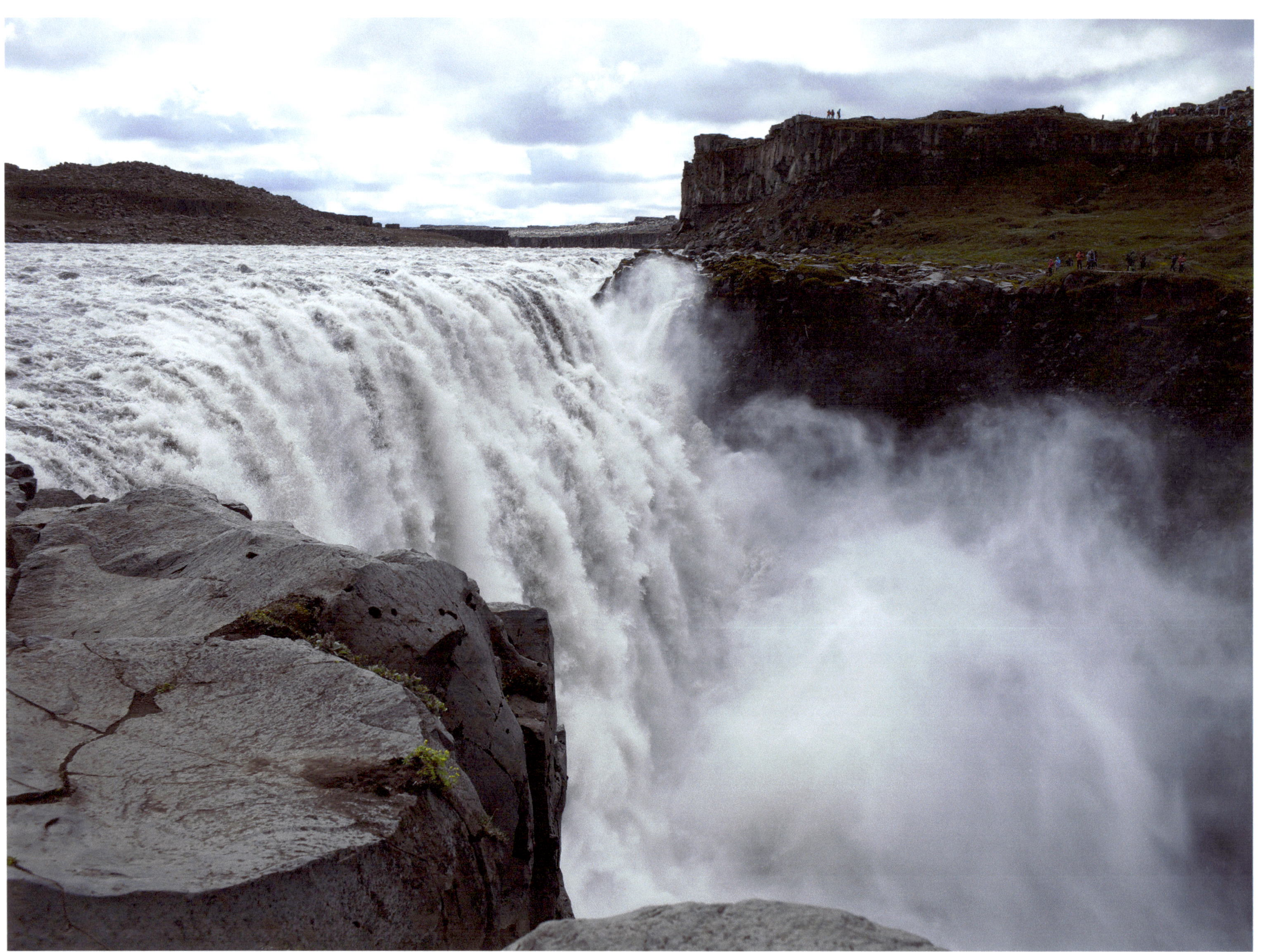

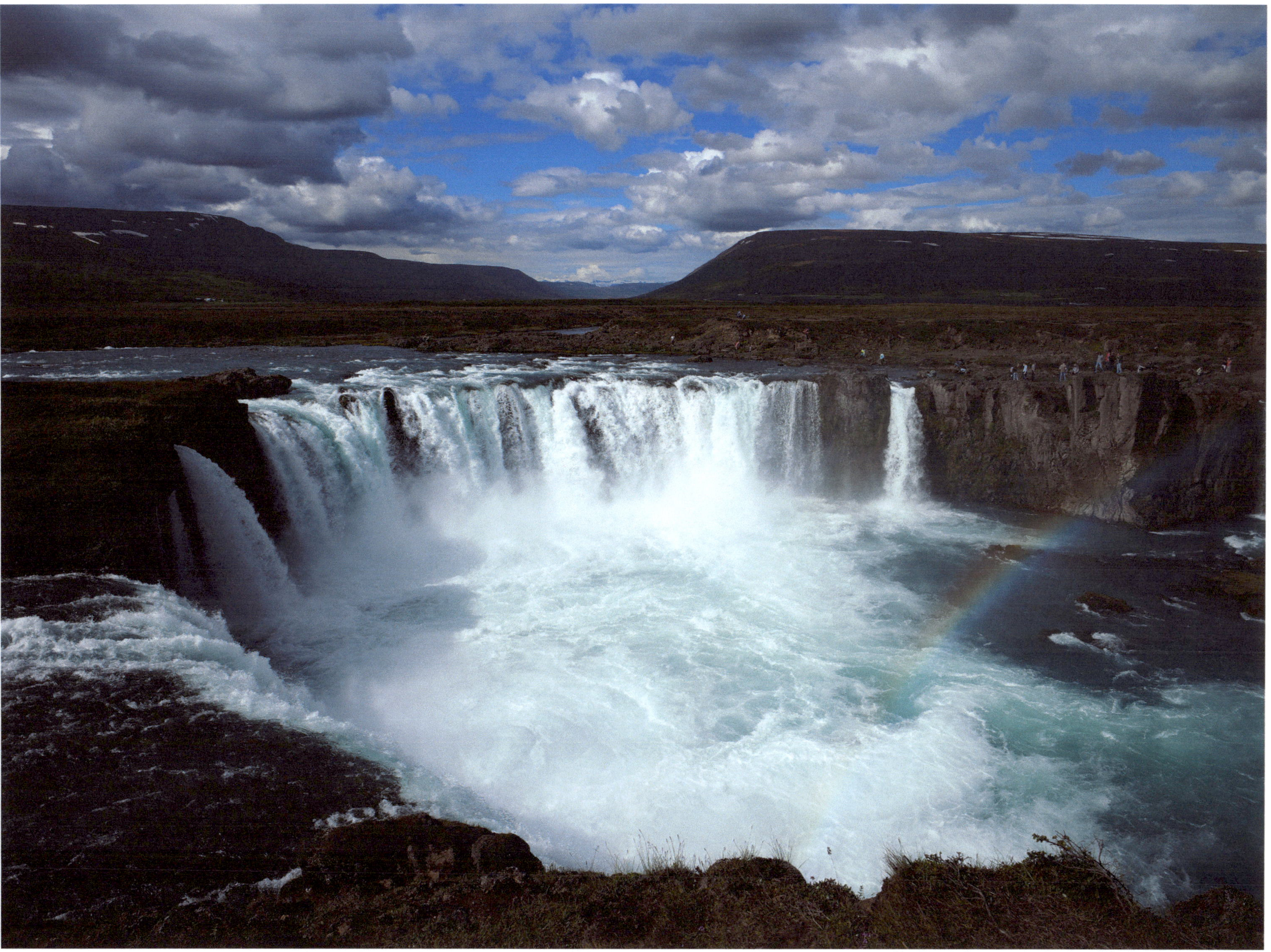

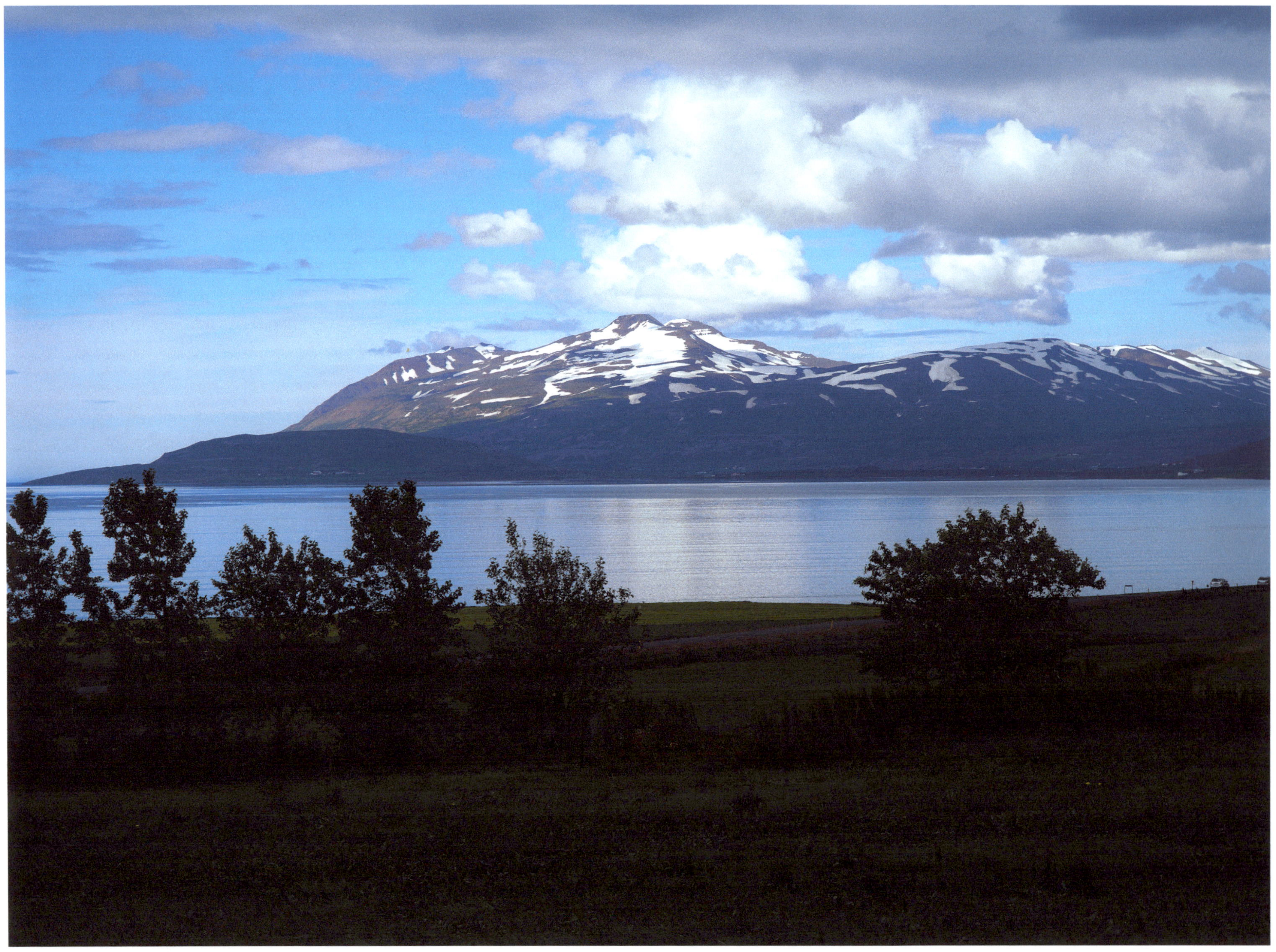

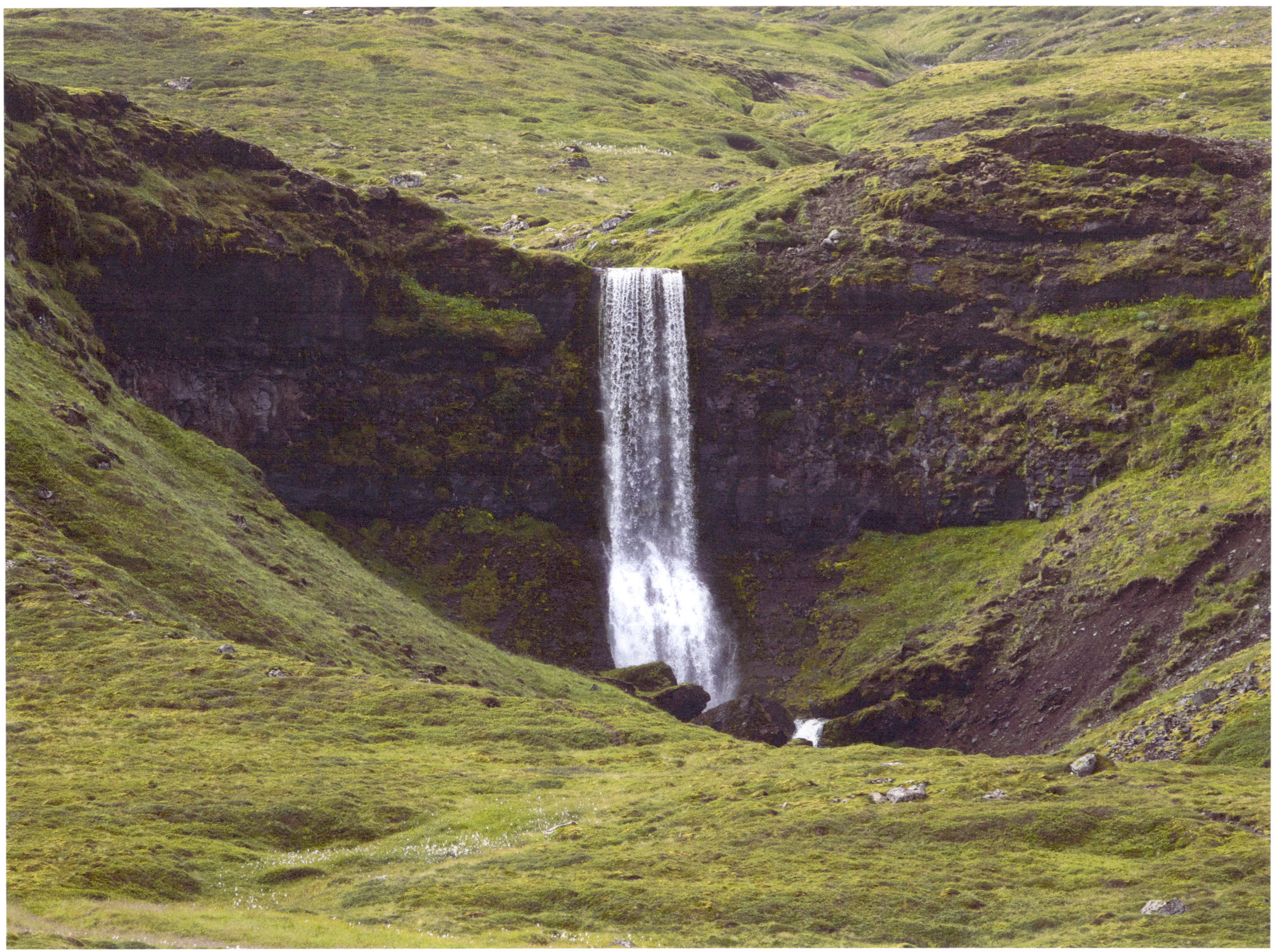

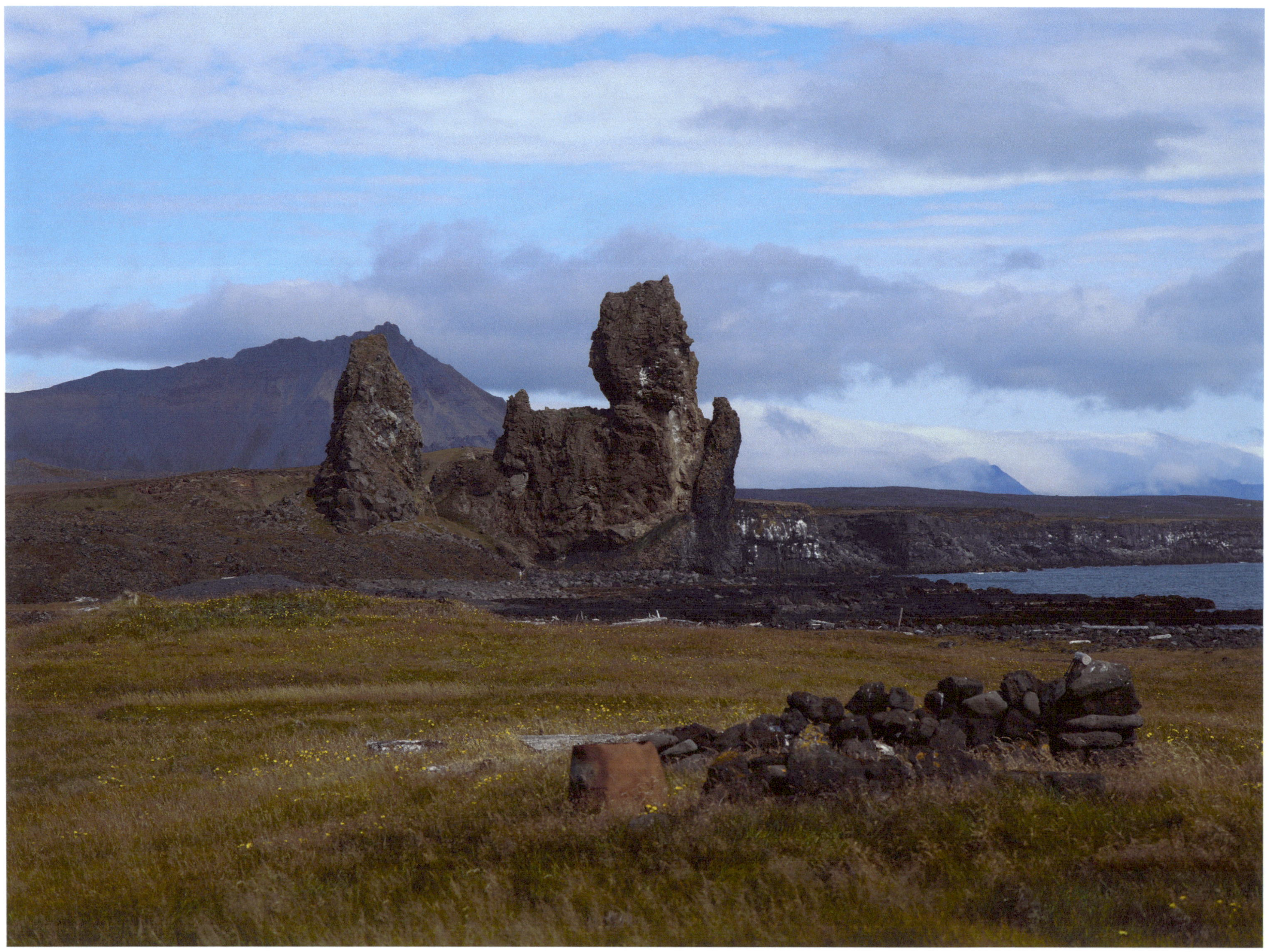

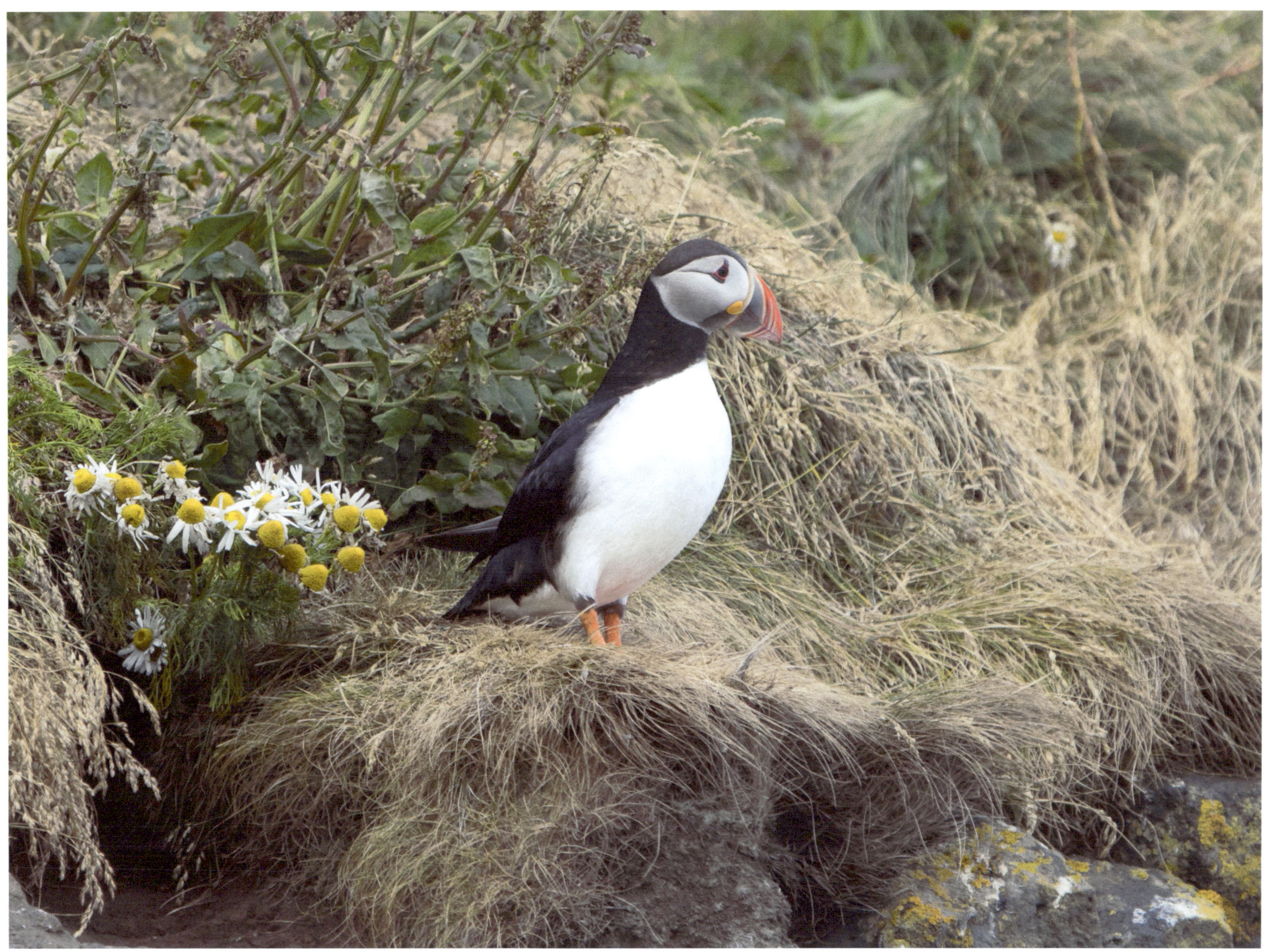

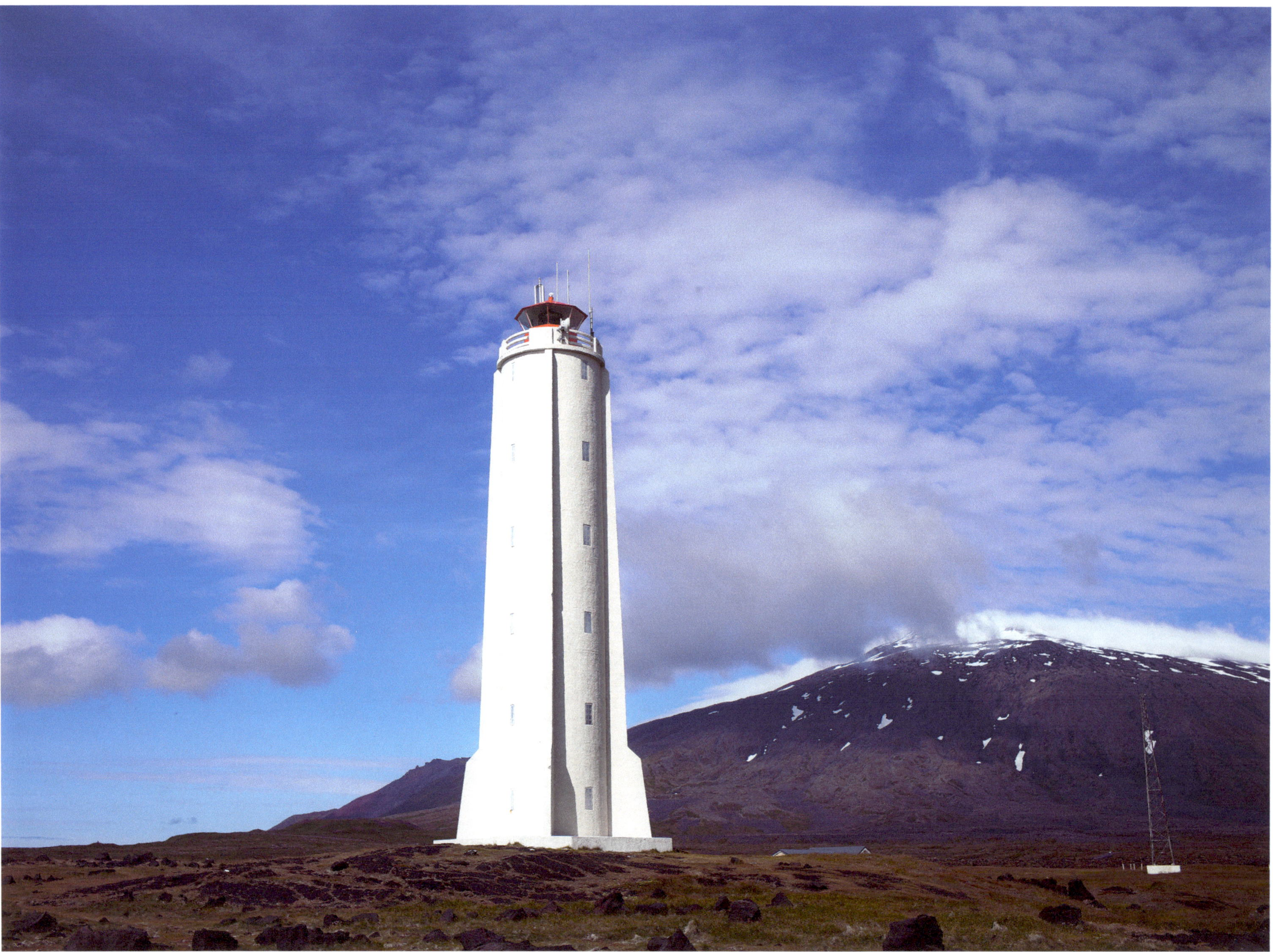

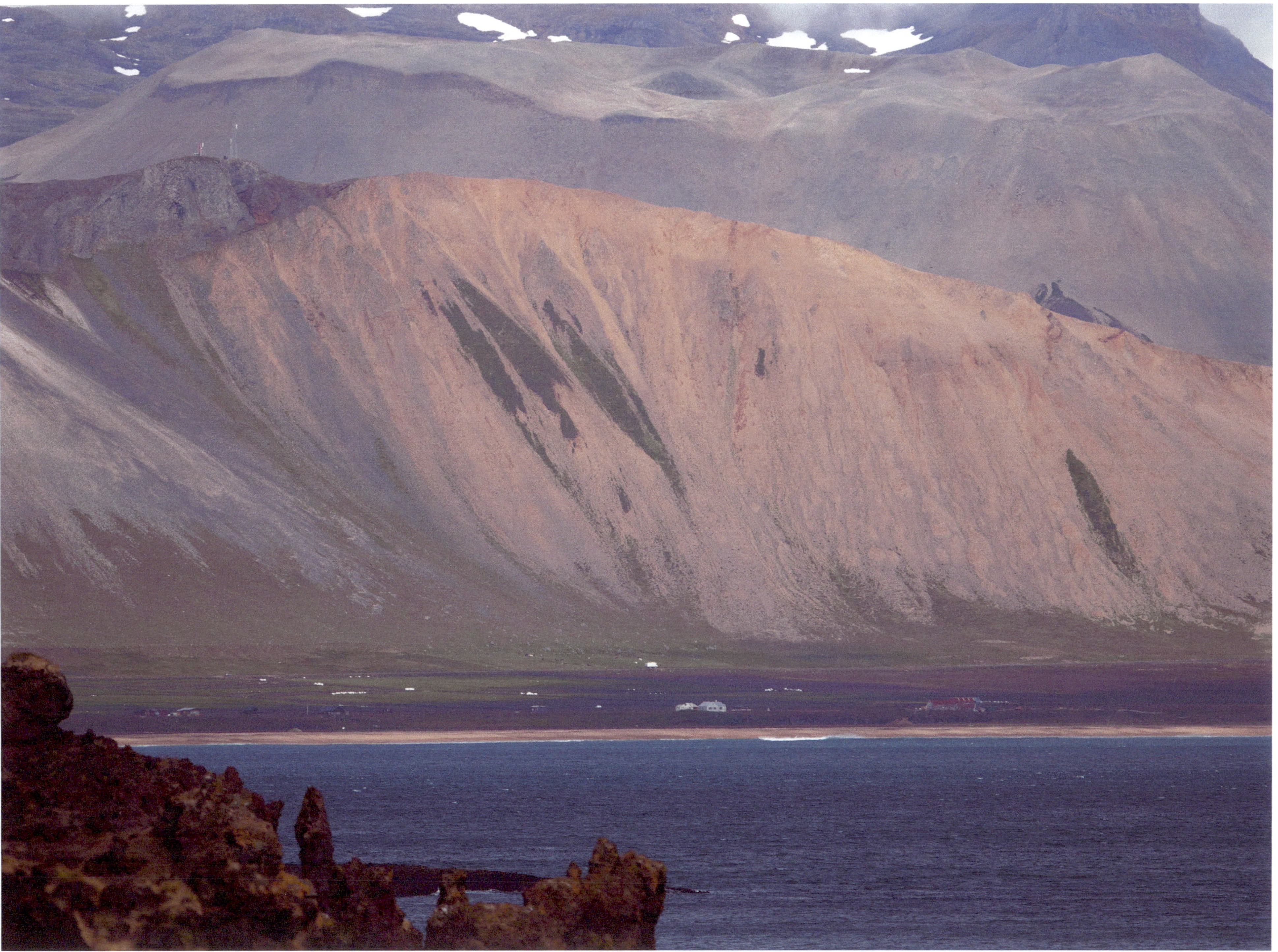

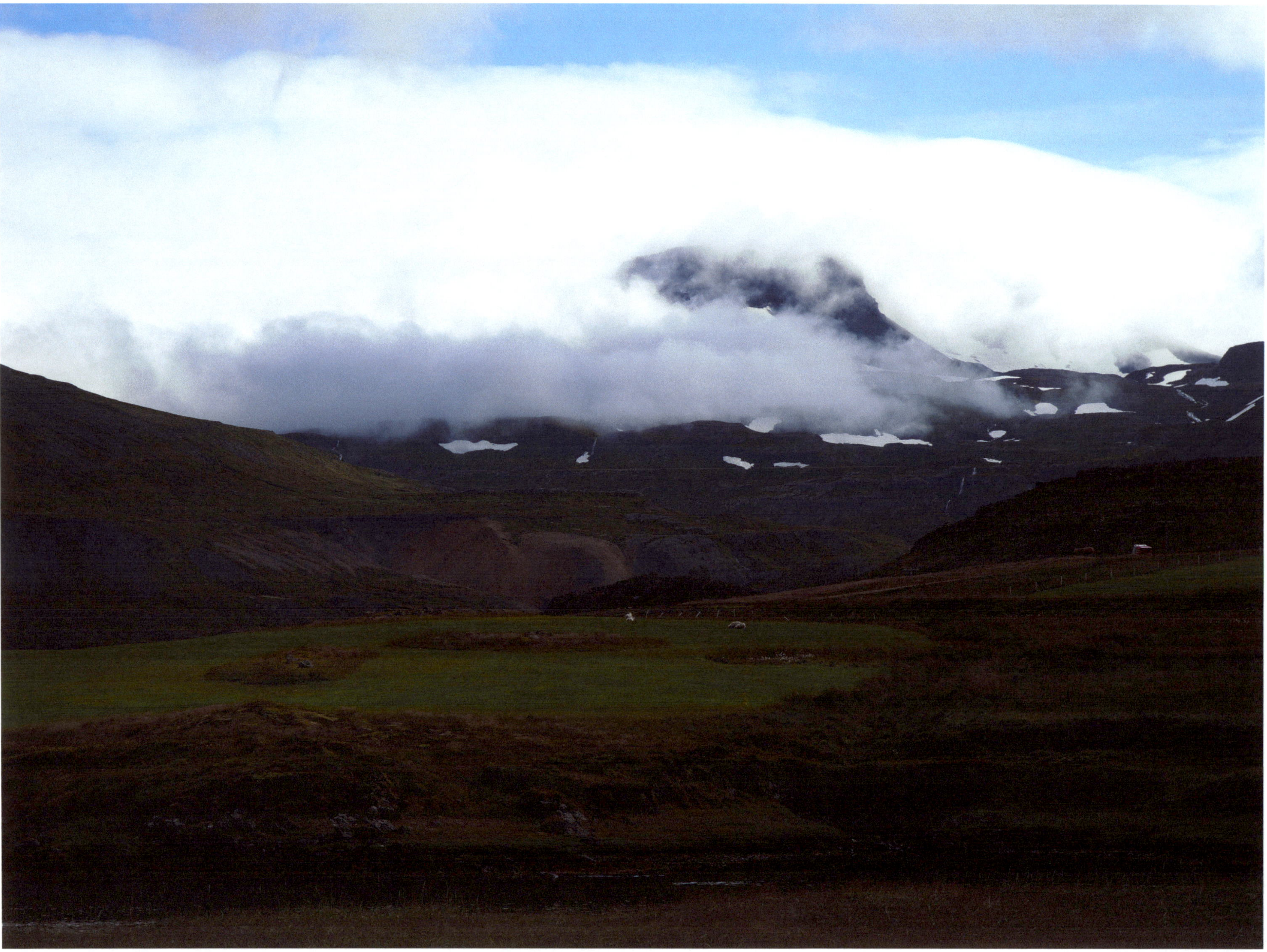

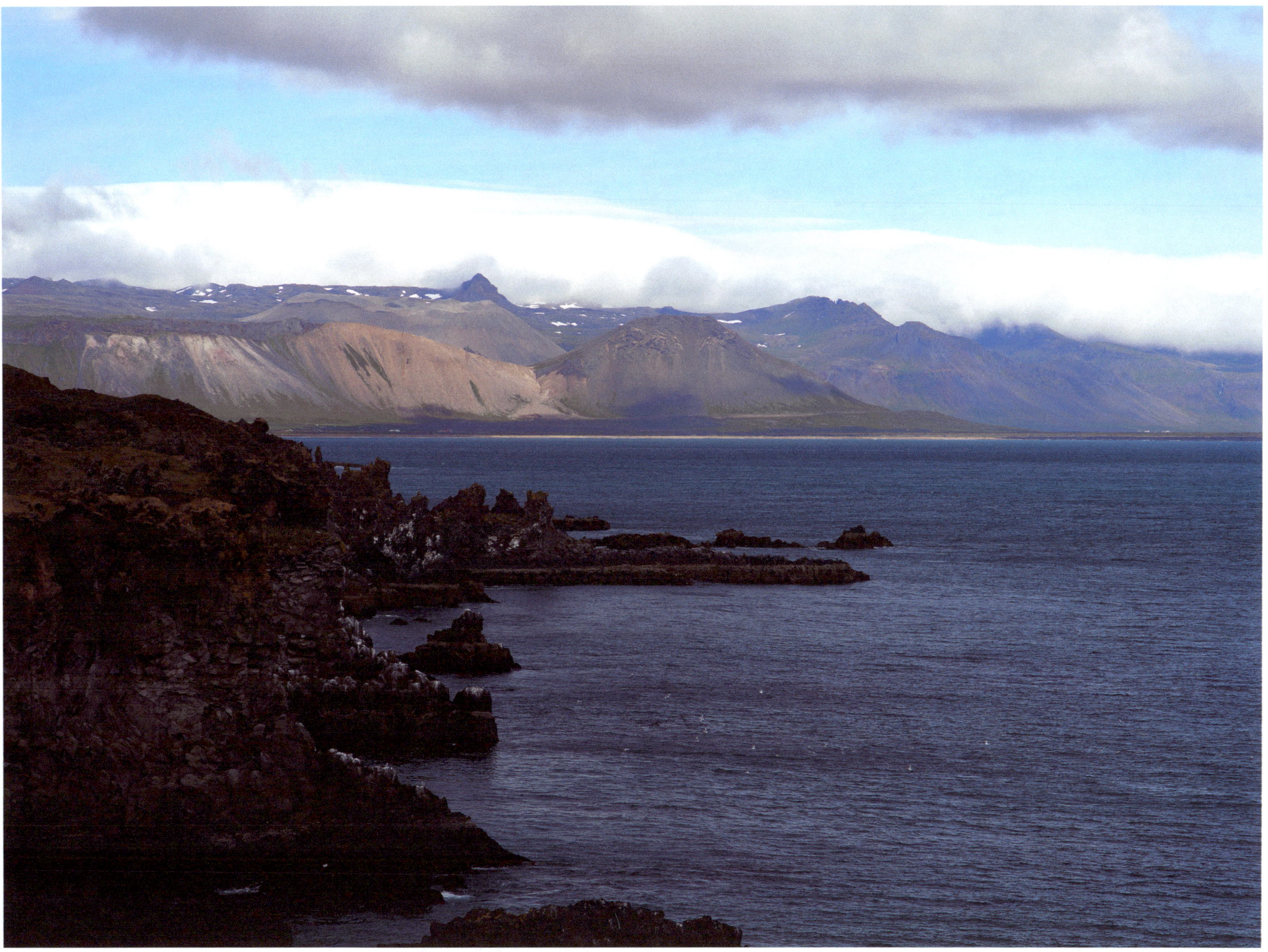

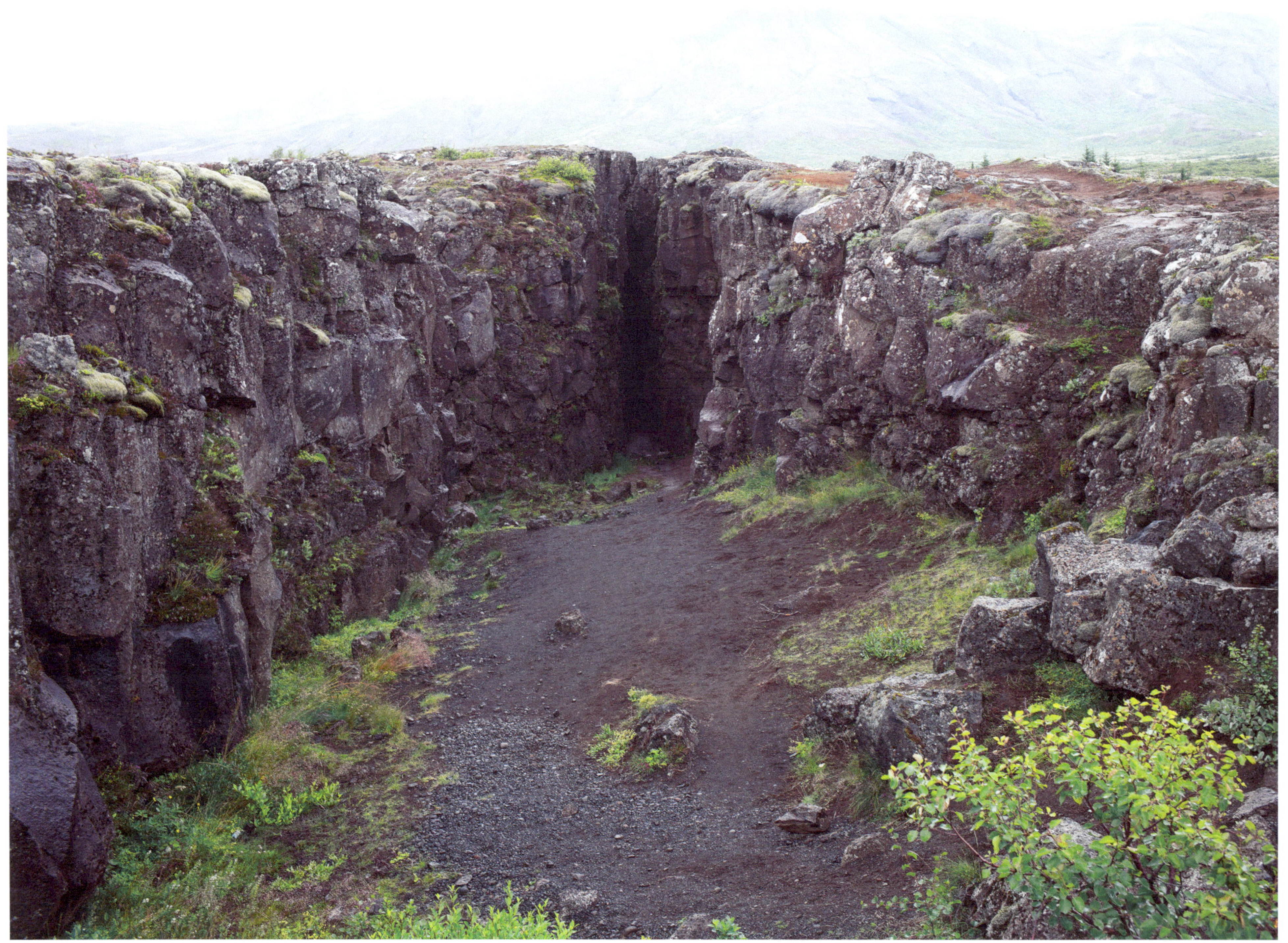

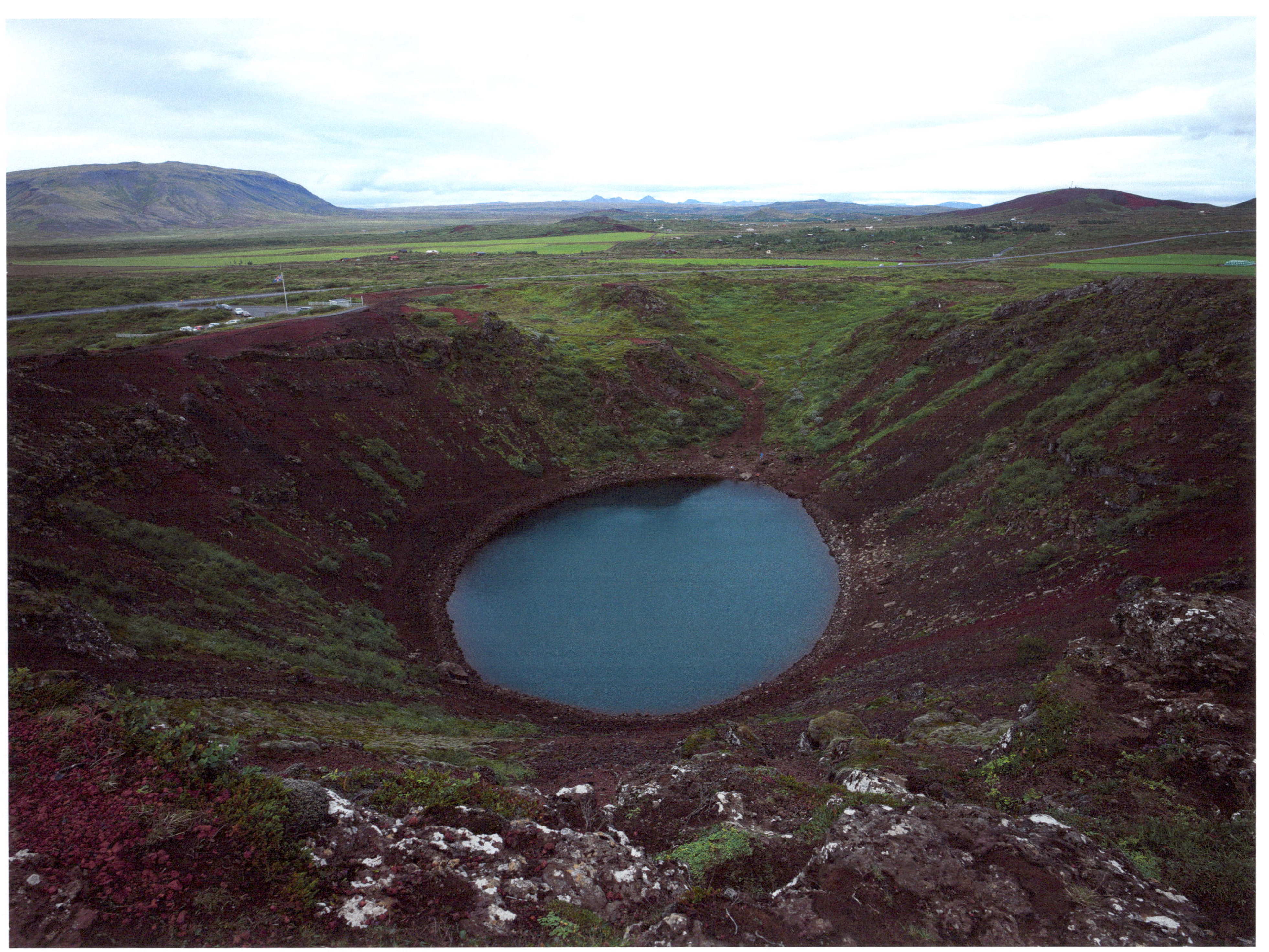

www.ingramcontent.com/pod-product-compliance
Lightning Source LLC
LaVergne TN
LVHW072331100826
845154LV00009B/151

* 9 7 8 0 9 7 1 0 7 0 2 8 8 *